THE EDINBURGH LITERARY GUIDE

Richard Demarco '92

THE BURNS MONUMENT FROM
CLARINDAS GRAVE IN
CANONGATE CHURCHYARD.

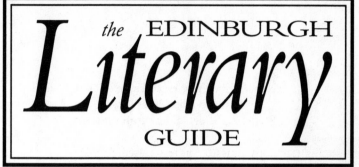

ANDREW LOWNIE

Illustrated by
Richard Demarco

CANONGATE PRESS

First published in Great Britain in 1992
by Canongate Press Plc,
14 Frederick Street, Edinburgh EH2 2HB.

Illustrations © Richard Demarco 1992

Richard Demarco dedicates the illustrations commissioned
for this book to his friend and mentor Bert Davies.

British Library Cataloguing-in-Publication Data
A catalogue record for this book is available from the
British Library.

ISBN 86241 360 5

Typeset by Hewer Text Composition Services, Edinburgh.
Printed and bound in Great Britain by
Dotesios Ltd, Trowbridge

Contents

Acknowledgements

Anyone writing about Edinburgh and its literary associations owes much to certain writers, most notably Alan Bold, Malcolm Cant, E. F. Catford, David Daiches, Owen Dudley Edwards, Alan Hamilton, Charles Smith and especially Trevor Royle. I have used their books extensively and my first thanks must go to them.

A number of other people offered useful comments while I was writing the book, in particular Andrew and Jean Davies. The staff at the Edinburgh Room of the Central Public Library were very patient and helpful during countless visits.

At Canongate my thanks go to Stephanie Wolfe Murray, Neville Moir and to my editors John Beaton and Duncan McAra. Last, but not least, I am grateful to my family for their support and judicious editing over the course of many drafts.

A. L.

Preface

Edinburgh's literary associations are so numerous, and her citizens often so possessive and knowledgeable about their history, that I should first of all explain my choice of material, in anticipation of any criticism.

This is not a definitive guide to Edinburgh's literary connections, merely a personal selection. I have been quite subjective concentrating on the last two hundred years and, indulging my own loves, like Stevenson and Garioch, while largely ignoring important, but now little read, writers like William Dunbar and Gavin Douglas.

I have tried to strike a balance between anecdote and narrative, and between those individuals who by virtue of birth, upbringing, residence or the subject matter of their work can be classed as 'Edinburgh writers' and the many visitors, who if not influenced in their work by Edinburgh, have at least responded to the city.

Over a hundred literary figures have been covered in the following pages and it has not always been possible to fully describe them or assess their importance, outside the confines of their relationship with Edinburgh.

Several hundred novels have taken the city as their backdrop and I have therefore also tried to give a flavour of some of them, and how writers have attempted to write about a capital that can be paradoxical and inscrutable. As such I hope this is not just a literary companion or guide but also a portrait of the city as seen by writers over the ages.

LADY STAIRS CLOSE, LAWNMARKET   RICHARD DEMARCO

The Old Town

The train swung into the flat lands of the Lothians and as we hurtled at sixty-five miles an hour through fields of hidden grain I glimpsed the small hill behind which was Bernard's home. Soon the speed slackened and we were on the outskirts of Edinburgh, with Arthur's Seat looming larger until we skirted its base and plunged into the defile of scruffy tenements and squalid sideroads that are the preamble to the largest, dirtiest and gloomiest station in Britain—Waverley.[1]
Neil McCallum *Scream in the Sky* (1964)

Waverley is for many visitors their first experience of Edinburgh. In a city rich in literary associations it is appropriate that the station should be named after Walter Scott's famous series of novels, and that it is the Gothic monument to Scott on Princes Street that first greets the traveller leaving the station.[2]

In few other major European cities is one brought so abruptly right to the heart of a city. Steep steps to the north of the station, often regarded as the windiest spot in Britain, lead to the principal shopping thoroughfare, Princes Street. Alternatively the western exit takes the visitor almost straight into Princes Street Gardens, an oasis of carefully manicured lawns in the shadow of the Castle.

To the south is Edinburgh's famous 'crag and tail' skyline which stretches from west to east—the colourful harl of Ramsay Garden, the foreboding exterior of the Divinity School, the magnificence of the Bank of Scotland, the jumble of the High Street tenements. To the north are the elegant, symmetrical streets of the New Town.

It is the Castle, however, that one notices first. Early in the morning its menacing presence looms out of the dark, at noon the sun may play upon its stonework casting giant shadows on the gardens below, while at night with lights blazing it stands out like some fairy castle above the city. At whatever time of day the Castle dominates the city's skyline:

> In every point of view, however, the main centre of attraction is the Castle of Edinburgh. From whatever side you approach the city—whether by water or by land—whether your foreground consists of height or of plain, of heath, of trees, or of the buildings of the city itself—this gigantic rock lifts itself high above all that surrounds it, and breaks upon the sky with the same commanding blackness of mingled crags, cliffs, buttresses, and battlements. These, indeed, shift and vary their outlines at every step, but everywhere there is the same unmoved effect of general expression—the same lofty and imposing image.[3]

Even when the haar, a raw mist, occasionally creeps in from the North Sea, and the Castle is shrouded from sight, its presence is detectable, providing a fixed point around which its citizens revolve. From almost anywhere in Edinburgh it can be seen in all its chameleon splendour. Glimpsed at night from King's Stables Road, silhouetted against the moon it seems like something from another century. However obscured, it is the heart and soul of Edinburgh.

The American writer, Washington Irving, on a visit to Walter Scott in 1817, wrote to his brother, Peter:

> It seemed as if the rock and castle assumed a new aspect every time I looked at them; and Arthur's Seat was perfect witchcraft. I don't wonder that anyone residing in Edinburgh should write poetically.[4]

The Castle also dominates the city's history. The Romans built a hill fort in order to protect the road from the south, and later invading armies from the south knew they had to capture it to retain control of the eastern part of Scotland. Gradually a settlement grew around it stretching down the volcanic overflow to create the present distinctive skyline.

The views from the Castle ramparts are spectacular: to the north, lie, in R. L. Stevenson's memorable phrase, the 'draughty parallelograms' of the New Town and, beyond,

EDINBURGH CASTLE & THE FLODDEN WALL   Richard Demarco '92

the gleaming waters of the Firth of Forth; to the south, the gentle undulations of the Pentland Hills; to the west, the suburbs spreading out past Corstorphine Hill; while to the east, lies the rolling farmland of East Lothian. It is this view that most attracts Iain, a young law apprentice, in Neil Gunn's novel *The Drinking Well*:

> Tilting over, like a bird in flight, his mind suddenly saw Princes Street. It was away below him, flat and wide; tramcars moved along it like automatic beetles and the people were dark points like black ants hurrying away but never leaving; yet the street itself was wide and full of air and princely. Behind the street were other streets, which, in the act of coming among them he knew intimately and with the momentary pleasure of surprise. Entrances to legal offices, insurance offices, brass plates, names, doors. Banking and accountancy. First floors and second floors and third floors. Lifts. Public Enquiries. Private inner doors and swing-door lavatories.[5]

It is a picture which has changed little in the ensuing years, save that the tramcars have been replaced by maroon or green buses, and some of the offices have moved down the hill into the Second New Town and further to the west. It is also a scene that emphasises the way the old and new Edinburgh co-exist so closely together.

The Castle's dramatic history has been widely reflected in literature. The Earl of Moray's famous climb up the north wall to recapture the Castle from the English in 1312, is described by Scott in *Tales from a Grandfather*, while there are a number of associations with Mary, Queen of Scots.

It was in a tiny room here in June 1566 that her son—the future James VI of Scotland and I of England—was born. There is much controversy about whether or not James really was a Stewart and a certain amount of evidence has been produced arguing that Mary's son died as an infant in the Borders, and the Countess of Mar's second son was substituted for the infant king. Certainly James shows few of the Stewart facial characteristics and bears a startling resemblance to John, Earl of Mar. In 1830 the legend was given a fresh twist when a small oak coffin was found within the wall of Mary's apartments in the castle containing the body of an infant wrapped in an embroidered silk covering bearing the letter J.[6]

During the Napoleonic Wars French prisoners were kept in the Castle. One can still see their graffiti carved on the stone walls of their cells and in the Scottish United Services Museum view the model ships they made to provide some income. The central figure of Stevenson's novel *St Ives* is one such French prisoner and he remembered how:

> Into the Castle of Edinburgh, standing in the midst of that city on the summit of an extraordinary rock, I was cast with several hundred fellow-sufferers, all privates like myself, and the more part of them, by an accident, very ignorant, plain fellows.[7]

The writer, George Borrow, was briefly quartered in the Castle about this time when his father, a Captain in the West Norfolk Militia, was posted there as adjutant. The Castle figures briefly at the beginning of Borrow's autobiographical novel *Lavengro*.[8]

One of the best known artifacts in the Castle stands in the French prisons. Forged in the fifteenth century, the power and range of Mons Meg was legendary, being able to fire a five-hundredweight stone at a target more than a mile and a half away. It burst in 1681, while firing a salute in honour of the Duke of York, later James VII, a disaster recorded by the poet, Robert Fergusson, who wrote:

> Oh willawins! Mons Meg for you,
> Twas firing crack'd thy muckle mou!

During the famous State visit of George IV to Scotland in 1822, Scott persuaded the king to return (in 1829) the magnificent siege cannon Mons Meg to the Castle from the Tower of London where it had been taken in 1754 in retaliation for the Porteous Riots. The history of the gun (now kept in the vaults of the French Prison) is given in a note to chapter 27 of Scott's *Rob Roy*.

Scott was also instrumental in the search for the traditional Scottish Regalia, otherwise known as the 'Honours

of Scotland'. These included the crown worn by Robert
Bruce, the sceptre and sword of state and the Order of the
Thistle. During the many centuries of war between England
and Scotland many attempts, none of them successful, had
been made to bring them to England.

At the time of the Act of Union in 1707 there were fears
they might at last be taken to England and again they were
hidden, this time in a huge chest in a vaulted chamber, which
was sealed up and instructions were left never to open the
door. There the 'Honours' remained for over a hundred years
until pressure from Scott and others led to the Crown Room
being opened in 1818 and the regalia being recovered. Scott's
son-in-law and biographer, J. G. Lockhart, leaves a moving
account of Scott's reaction on first seeing the 'Honours',
which are now on display in the Crown Room at the top
of the Castle.[9] For many writers the Castle is representative
of, and integral to, the city. Perhaps the most famous lines
about it come from Scott:

> Such dusky grandeur clothed the height
> Where the huge castle holds its state
> And all the steep slope down,
> Whose ridgy back heaves to the sky
> Piled deep and mossy, close and high
> Mine Own Romantic Town.

Eric Linklater (1899–1974), who was posted to the Castle
to join the Reserve Battalion of the Black Watch, after being
wounded during the First World War, has written about it
widely both in his book on Edinburgh and in several of his
novels. In *The Impregnable Women* the Castle is occupied by
women determined to stop the Second World War, while in
Magnus Merriman he gives a lyrical description of it:

> It is a castle of moods, now merely antiquated, now
> impregnable, now the work of giants and now of dreams;
> a fairy castle, a haunted castle, a castle in Spain, a castle you
> may enter with a twopenny guide book in your hand; it has
> heard the cry of Flodden, the travail of queens, the iron
> scuffle of armour . . . it is Scotland's castle, Queen Mary's

castle and the castle of fifty thousand annual visitors who walk through it with rain on their boots and bewilderment in their hearts.[10]

A number of Linklater's books or short stories have an Edinburgh setting. His story 'Kind Kitty', inspired by a poem of William Dunbar, concerns an old woman in the Edinburgh slums during the 1930s while perhaps his most popular 'Joy as it Flies' also has some Edinburgh scenes. His satirical novel *The Merry Muse* revolves around the discovery of sixteen hitherto unknown erotic poems by Robert Burns, and the effect this find has on a cross-section of the capital's citizens.

His close friend, Compton Mackenzie, dedicated *The East Wind of Love* to him. One of Linklater's sons, Andro, in turn became Mackenzie's biographer, while the eldest, Magnus, is editor of *The Scotsman*.

Linklater noted that it was while drilling on the Esplanade that his love for Edinburgh was first nurtured. Nowadays the best known drilling on the Esplanade takes place for the Military Tattoo during the Edinburgh International Festival. Huge stands suddenly fill the expanse, overhanging precariously over the gardens below, while the skirl of pipes can be heard through the cool night air. Several novels have at their centre plots to blow up the tattoo including *The Edinburgh Exercise* by Angus Ross and Owen John's *Festival*. The latter has a splendid description of a tattoo:

> At that moment a great roar came from the Esplanade; the crowd clapped and cheered, then silence fell over the Esplanade. The powerful searchlights swung to the high wall of Half Moon Battery. A line of soldiers stood to attention. In a sudden brilliant flash the bugles went to their mouths. A hush fell over the arena, all eyes turned towards the great, curved bastion.
>
> The buglers sounded a magnificent fanfare, which reached out from the Castle over the ancient city. In perfect unison the bugles filled the night with their call. Then they stopped. The lights went out. There was darkness. The fanfare was over. The crowds burst into enthusiastic clapping. The Military Tattoo had started.[11]

Leaving the Esplanade one comes to the Outlook Tower and a steep lane which leads to Ramsay Garden. Rebuilt in the 1890s by the town planner, Sir Patrick Geddes, the tall narrow flats, with their cross-slipped gables, are a familiar Edinburgh landmark and it is well worth the detour just to see the attractive window-box displays and cast-iron staircases.

In 1738 the poet, Allan Ramsay (1686–1758), built himself a retirement home here, which he called Ramsay Lodge. The house was promptly dubbed the 'Goose Pie', because of its strange octagonal shape. Ramsay, one of the most important early literary figures in the city's history, was born in Lanarkshire but came to Edinburgh in his teens to be apprenticed to a wig-maker. In 1712 he opened his own wig shop in the Grassmarket and also founded the Easy Club, a society for 'mutual improvement in Conversation'.

His first collection of poetry, published in 1721, did much to restore interest in an earlier Scottish literary tradition. This was followed in 1724 by the first of his five volumes of '*The Tea-Table Miscellany*', a collection of Scots songs and ballads. A great many of Ramsay's poems celebrate his love of Edinburgh's low life, and in particular the taverns and brothels of the High Street.

By this time Ramsay had abandoned wig-making for a career as a bookseller and publisher in Niddry's Wynd, where he wrote *The Gentle Shepherd*; the play, a simply constructed story of life in the Pentland Hills, was an influence on later Scottish poetry. Ramsay spent the final years of his life at the 'Goose Pie' House and on his death it passed to his son, the portrait painter Allan Ramsay.

Returning up Ramsay Lane one comes to the top of the High Street. Daniel Defoe on his tour of Scotland in 1724 called it 'the largest, longest, and finest street for Buildings and Number of Inhabitants, not in Bretain only, but in the World', a view shared by the English traveller, Edward Topham, in his *Letters from Edinburgh* in 1774.

As the population of Edinburgh grew, shortage of space within the city walls meant that the houses or tenements became increasingly taller, giving the High Street its distinct appearance. This shortage of space also led to the various social groups living in close proximity, and even on top of each other, with the result that not only was Edinburgh the first city with multi-storey flats but from its very beginnings one where the social classes easily mixed.

With the construction of the first part of the New Town in the mid-eighteenth century the more prosperous tended to move out so that by the mid-nineteenth century the tenements had become slum areas.

The central figure in William Boyd's novel *The New Confessions*, John James Todd, was brought up in one of these tenements at the beginning of the twentieth century:

> Some of these old buildings contained up to twenty apartments, some small, some grand. Ours was one of the latter; I think at one stage two had been knocked into one. There was a large drawing room, a library, a dining room, six bedrooms and a bathroom. A large kitchen with a pantry, a scullery, and a sleeping closet constituted the servant's quarters. There had been buildings on this site since the fifteenth century. From time to time they had fallen or burnt down and new dwellings had been constructed on the ruins. The architecture on the High Street had the character of an antiquated, stone shanty town. Houses had grown piecemeal, by accretion and alteration. Windows were all sizes—actually a pleasing diversity—and installing water closets and modern plumbing required real ingenuity.[12]

A few yards down the High Street on the north side is a narrow passage which leads into James Court, one of the last additions to the Old Town. An open square built by James Brownhill between 1723 and 1727, much of it was destroyed by a fire in 1857. Only an eight-storey building in the north-east corner survives. It is perhaps fitting that one of the linking figures between the Union and the Scottish Enlightenment should have lived here. A plaque records that the philosopher David Hume lived in the court between 1762 and 1782. It is thought he had a flat on the third floor of the western block.

Hume (1711–76) was born in Edinburgh and briefly studied law at the University but finding it 'nauseous' turned to a wider course of reading to prepare himself, as he put it, to be 'a Scholar & Philosopher'. In 1734 he left for London and then Paris where he wrote perhaps his best-known book, the *Treatise of Human Nature* (1739), in which he first advanced his arguments about the importance of reason.

After several diplomatic posts abroad, Hume returned to Edinburgh in 1751, living first at Riddle's Court, where he wrote his *Political Discourses* (1752), and then Jack's Land, both further down the High Street. His final address in the city was at the corner of St Andrew Square and South St David Street. He is commemorated by a monument in the Old Calton Burying Ground and the University's David Hume Tower. Ironically he was twice passed over for university professorships, because of his religious scepticism, and many, including Dr Johnson, refused to meet him.

It is perhaps just as well that they did not meet, though they so easily could have, for Hume rented his flat to James Boswell (1740–95). It was in James Court that Boswell entertained Samuel Johnson (1709–84) on the Doctor's famous visit to Edinburgh in 1773. Johnson spent four days in the city before heading north. His first impressions of Edinburgh were not good. Boswell tells us that on arrival Johnson had asked for his lemonade to be sweetened, whereupon the waiter 'lifted a lump of sugar with his greasy fingers' and put it in the drink. The outraged Doctor threw the offending drink out of the window.

The practice of discarding one's waste was not unique to Johnson. The cry of 'Gardyloo', a corruption of the French 'Garde de l'eau', was often to be heard as slops were hurled from the tenement windows to the street below.

The city's dirtiness was one of the principal memories Daniel Defoe (1660–1731) had when he visited Edinburgh in 1724:

> The City suffers infinite Disadvantages, and lies under such scandalous Inconveniences as are, by its Enemies, made a Subject of Scorn and Reproach; as if the People were not as willing to live sweet and clean as other Nations, but delighted in Stench and Nastiness: whereas, were any other People to live under the same Unhappiness, I mean

BOSWELL'S · COURT ·

3522

THE WITCHERY

JAMES BOSWELL
DR. SAMUEL JOHNSON

Boswell's court, Castlehill   Richard Demarco

as well of a rocky and mountainous Situation, throng'd
Buildings, from seven to ten or twelve story high, a
Scarcity of Water, and that little they have difficult to
be had, and to the uppermost Lodgings, far to fetch; we
should find a *London* or a *Bristol* as dirty as *Edinburgh*, and,
perhaps, less able to make their Dwelling tolerable, at least
in so narrow a Compass; for, tho' many cities have more
People in them, yet, I believe, this may be said with Truth,
that in no City in the World so many People live in so little
Room as at *Edinburgh*.[13]

James Court leads into Lady Stair's Close, named after
Elizabeth Dowager Countess of Stair, a leader of Edinburgh
Society in the seventeenth century and noted for being the
first person to keep a black servant.

However it is with her daughter-in-law Eleanor that the
Close is most clearly associated. Eleanor's first husband was
Lord Primrose, who so ill-treated both her and their four
children that when it was discovered he was forced to flee
the country. One day Eleanor consulted a foreign fortune
teller and is supposed to have seen in a mirror that Primrose
had married bigamously. As she watched she saw her brother
enter and draw his sword to prevent the marriage, whereupon
the vision faded. Soon after her brother confirmed that what
she had seen was true. The story made a strong impression
on Sir Walter Scott who used it as the basis of his story *My
Aunt Margaret's Mirror*.

On the death of Primrose in 1706 she resolved not to marry
again though still a young and attractive woman. The Earl of
Stair declined to accept her refusals of marriage, and when all
persuasion failed he secreted himself in her house, and showed
himself half-dressed at her window in the morning. How far
this slur to her reputation affected her decision is not known,
but she married him shortly afterwards.

A plaque at the entrance to the Close commemorates the
visit of Robert Burns (1759–96) in 1786. Burns had come to
Edinburgh following the success of his first collection, *Poems
Chiefly in the Scottish Dialect*, published in Kilmarnock three
months earlier. He stayed in lodgings kept by a Mrs Carfrae,
'a staid sober piously-disposed skuldudery-abhoring widow',

in what was then Baxter's Close and now corresponds to the east side of Lady Stair's Close. Burns had been given an introduction to the Earl of Glencairn and soon he was the toast of Edinburgh society. It was Glencairn who persuaded the Caledonian Hunt to subscribe 100 copies of this Edinburgh edition, for which Burns was paid 100 guineas for the copyright. The Edinburgh edition includes his 'Address to Edinburgh'.

> Edina! Scotia's darling seat,
> All hail thy palaces and tow'rs,
> Where once, beneath a Monarch's feet,
> Sat Legislation's's sov'reign pow'rs.

It is perhaps fitting given all these associations that Lady Stair's House should now house a museum, which is well worth visiting, devoted to probably the three most important writers connected with Edinburgh—Robert Burns, Sir Walter Scott and Robert Louis Stevenson.

Deacon Brodie, one of Edinburgh's best known characters, lived in Brodie's Court. His house has now gone, and the closest memorial is Deacon Brodie's Tavern opposite, situated at 435 Lawnmarket. William Brodie was by day a respected cabinet-maker and locksmith and member of the Town Council, but at night could generally be found nearby, either at the Cape Club in Craig's Close or James Clarke's Tavern at the head of Fleshmarket Close. There he would drink, gamble and indulge his mistresses.

Such pursuits did not come cheap and in 1786 he decided to turn to a life of crime. For two years he was responsible for a series of robberies around Edinburgh until in March 1788 he, and his accomplices, were surprised while attempting to break into the General Excise Office for Scotland in Chessel's Court. They managed to escape, Brodie making his way south to Dover and the Continent. However he was betrayed when one of his colleagues turned King's Evidence and was traced through letters he had sent to his mistress. He was brought back, tried by Lord Braxfield (the inspiration for Stevenson's Weir of Hermiston) and executed that October near to St Giles on a gallows of his own design.

"THE SCOTSMAN" BUILDING IN
FLESHMARKET CLOSE   Richard Demarco 9

Stevenson was fascinated by him and wrote a play with W. E. Henley called *Deacon Brodie or The Double Life* (1880), while Muriel Spark in *The Prime of Miss Jean Brodie* (1961) makes her central character, a woman herself torn between her repressed nature and romantic longings, a direct descendant of the cabinet-maker. G. K. Chesterton has argued convincingly that Stevenson's *The Strange Case of Dr Jeykll and Mr Hyde* owes more to Edinburgh than its ostensible setting of London[14].

Matthew Bramble writing to Dr Lewis in Tobias Smollett's novel *The Expedition of Humphry Clinker* noted:

> All the people of busines at Edinburgh, and even the genteel company, may be seen standing in crowds every day, from one to two in the afternoon, in the open street, at a place where formerly stood a market-cross, which (by the bye) was a curious piece of Gothic architecture . . .[15]

This was the Mercat Cross where bankrupts were brought, merchants met and crowds gathered to hear the news and exchange gossip. It was also for a time the place of execution. According to the legend preserved in Scott's *Marmion*, it was at the Mercat Cross that the names of those doomed at the Battle of Flodden were given, even before news of the defeat was brought to the citizens of Edinburgh.

Nearby, in the centre of Parliament Square, is a statue of Charles II on horseback. It was placed there in 1685 on the site of the old St Giles graveyard, where John Knox was buried. By a stroke of irony, therefore, the Merry Monarch prances on the remains of the Gloomy Reformer.

The Advocates' Library in Parliament House was founded in 1689 by Sir George Mackenzie of Rosehaugh (1636–91), and became the basis of the National Library of Scotland. Mackenzie, who wrote a number of books on political matters, is credited with writing the first novel published in Scotland, *Aretina* (1660), a pastoral romance set in Egypt. As Lord Advocate he was responsible for prosecuting the Covenanters and appears as 'Bluidy Mackenzie' in Walter Scott's *Old Mortality*.

Parliament Hall is entered by the doorway on the south

side of Parliament Square. It is an impressive sight: 122 ft long, 49 ft wide with a 60 ft roof of dark oaken beams with cross-braces and hammer-beams resting on curiously-carved corbels. At the south end there is a huge stained-glass window depicting the inauguration of the Court of Session and College of Justice by James V in May 1532.

Apart from Mondays it is filled with advocates in their gowns and wigs pacing its length in consultation either with clients or their solicitors. A statue of Sir Walter Scott looks benignly down on the proceedings. Thomas Carlyle on his first visit to Edinburgh in November 1809 was noticeably struck by it:

> An immense Hall, dimly lighted from the top of the walls, and perhaps with candles burning in it here and there; all in strange 'chiaroscuro', and filled with what I thought (exaggeratively) a thousand or two of human creatures; all astir in a boundless buzz of talk, and simmering about in every direction, some solitary, some in groups. By degrees I noticed that some were in wig and black gown, some not, but in common clothes, all well-dressed; that here and there on the sides of the Hall, were little thrones with enclosures, and steps leading up; red-velvet figures sitting in said thrones, and the black-gowned eagerly speaking to them,—Advocates pleading to Judges, as I easily understood. How they could be heard in such a grinding din was somewhat a mystery. Higher up on the walls, stuck there like swallows in their nests, sat other humbler figures: these I found were the sources of certain wildly plangent lamentable kinds of sounds or echoes which from time to time pierced the universal noise of feet and voices, and rose unintelligibly above it, as if in the bitterness of incurable woe;—Criers of the Court, I gradually came to understand.[16]

Stevenson, who had spent many unhappy hours there, while training to be a lawyer, was less complimentary:

> A pair of swing doors gives admittance to a hall with a carved roof, hung with legal portraits, adorned with legal statuary, lighted by windows of painted glass, and warmed

ADVOCATE'S CLOSE.   Richard Demarco '92

by three vast fires. This is the 'Salle des pas perdus' of the Scottish Bar. Here, by a ferocious custom, idle youths must promenade from ten till two. From end to end, singly or in pairs or trios, the gowns and wigs go back and forward. Through a hum of talk and footfalls, the piping tones of a Macer announce a fresh cause and call upon the names of those concerned. Intelligent men have been walking here daily for ten or twenty years without a rag of business or a shilling of reward. . . .[17]

Stevenson had qualified as a lawyer at the insistence of his father, who felt he should have some qualification to fall back on if his writing did not prosper. Stevenson did not waste his experience for many of his characters are lawyers: Prestongrange, Rankeillor, Stewart, Utterson, Mr Johnstone Thomson WS, the 'hanging judge' Weir.

The law plays an important part in Edinburgh life and there is a long tradition of lawyers also being Men of Letters. Lawyers often worked for only six months of the year and Henry, Lord Cockburn, himself a judge and journalist, thought it was 'this abstraction from legal business that has given Scotland the greater part of literature that has adorned her. The lawyers have been the most intellectual class in the country.'

Writers with strong legal connections include Francis Jeffrey, founder of the *Edinburgh Review* and Lord Advocate; James Boswell, who was a practising barrister; David Hume for many years Keeper of the Faculty of Advocates; and Sir Walter Scott, Clerk to the Court of Session between 1806 and 1830.

Many of Scott's novels have scenes set around the Law Courts, a tradition continued to this day in novels such as *The Justice-Clerk* by W. D. Lyell, *A Judge of Men* by James Allan Ford (himself a former Registrar General for Scotland) and *The Hermitage* by Magda Sweetland[18].

According to J. G. Lockhart's *Peter's Letters to his Kinsfolk*:

The western side of the quadrangle is occupied in all its length by the Church of St Giles's, which in the later times of Scottish Episcopacy possessed the dignity of a Cathedral, and which, indeed, has been the scene of many of the most remarkable incidents in the ecclesiastical history of Scotland. In its general exterior, this church presents by no means a fine specimen of the Gothic architecture, although there are several individual parts about the structure which display great beauty—the tower above all which rises out of the centre of the pile, and is capped with a very rich and splendid canopy in the shape of a Crown Imperial. This beautiful tower and canopy form a fine point in almost every view of the city of Edinburgh; but the effect of the whole building, when one hears and thinks of it as a Cathedral, is a thing of no great significance.[19]

Lockhart is perhaps a little unfair. The High Kirk of St Giles does dominate Parliament Square. St Giles was originally the Parish Church of Edinburgh and its history can be traced back to the twelfth century. One of Edinburgh's earliest writers Gavin Douglas (1474–1522), who translated the *Aeneid* into Middle Scots, was Provost for a time. The church has been considerably rebuilt over the centuries, with a final restoration in the 1870s.

Lockhart in the extract refers to its short period (1633–1638; 1661–89) as an Episcopal Cathedral. This took place after the famous, and probably fictitious, stool-throwing episode of Jenny Geddes who was opposed to the introduction of the Book of Common Prayer and one of the religious reforms of Charles I that the Scots opposed.

There are a number of literary memorials inside the High Kirk. Beneath the oriel window in the west wall is a large memorial bronze to Stevenson by Augustus St Gaudens which pays tribute to Stevenson's 'spirit of mirth, courage and love' and quotes his 'Requiem' with its concluding words:

> Here he lies where he longed to be;
> Home is the sailor, home from sea;
> And the hunter home from the hill.

In the original version of the memorial the right hand holds a cigarette, but a pen was thought more appropriate in a Kirk.

The central west window, designed by Leifur Breidfjord, a former student at the Edinburgh College of Art, was dedicated in 1985 as a tribute to Robert Burns.

Muriel Spark in *The Prime of Miss Jean Brodie* uses St Giles to personify the Scots' former preoccupation with the Calvinistic theory of the Elect. Sandy, the only girl to eventually see through Jean Brodie's division of the world into the *crème de la crème* and the rest, is frightened by St Giles:

> with its tattered blood-stained banners of the past. Sandy had not been there, and did not want to go. The outskirts of old Edinburgh churches frightened her, they were of such dark stone, like presences against the colour of the castle rock, and were built so warningly with their upraised fingers.[20]

Another passage perhaps spells out more clearly what Calvinism means:

> Fully to savour her position, Sandy would go and stand outside St Giles Cathedral or the Tolbooth, and contemplate these emblems of a dark and terrible salvation which made the fires of the damned seem very merry to the imagination by contrast, and much preferable. Nobody in her life, at home or at school, had ever spoken of Calvinism except as a joke that had once been taken seriously.[21]

A heart-shaped pattern of cobblestones known as the Heart of Midlothian next to St Giles marks the position of the doorway of the Tolbooth. Consisting of three buildings, the first of which was built in the mid-fifteenth century, it served in turn as the meeting place of the Scots Parliament, the Town Hall, chambers for the Privy Council and as the College of Justice. In 1640 it became a gaol for debtors and criminals and among those imprisoned there were the rebels of the first Jacobite Rising in 1715. In 1817 the gaol was pulled down to be replaced by a new gaol on Calton Hill. The prison's heavy wooden door was presented to Scott, and can still be seen at his house, Abbotsford, in the Borders.

Until their removal at the same time as that of the Tolbooth, much of the local trade was conducted in a

series of timber-fronted tenements of up to six storeys
that stretched along the north wall of St Giles. Matthew
Bramble in *The Expedition of Humphry Clinker* thought the
High Street:

> would be undoubtedly one of the noblest streets in Europe,
> if an ugly mass of mean buildings, called the Lucken-
> Booths, had not thrust itself, by what accident I know
> not, into the middle of the way, like Middle-Row in
> Holborn.[22]

This view was shared by Scott in his famous description
of the Luckenbooths in his novel *The Heart of Midlothian*:

> for some inconceivable reason, our ancestors had jammed
> into the middle of the principal street of the town, leaving
> for passage a narrow street on the north, and on the
> south, into which the prison opens, a narrow crooked
> lane, winding betwen the high and sombre walls of the
> Tolbooth and of the adjacent houses on one side, and
> the buttresses and projections of the old Church upon the
> other. To give some gaiety to this sombre passage (well
> known by the name of the Krames), a number of little
> booths or shops, after the fashion of cobblers' stalls, are
> plastered as it were against the Gothic projectments and
> abutments, so that it seemed as if the traders had occupied
> with nests bearing the same proportion to the building,
> every buttress and coign of vantage, as the martlet did
> in Macbeth's Castle. Of later years these booths have
> degenerated into mere toy shops . . . but at the time
> of which we write, hosiers, glovers, hatters, mercers,
> milliners, and all who dealt in the miscellaneous wares
> now termed 'haberdashers' goods,' were to be found in
> the narrow alley.[23]

Balfour, in Stevenson's *Catriona*, visits the Luckenbooths
to be fitted out so 'that servants should respect me'.

Allan Ramsay had his bookshop on the first floor of the
eastern Luckenbooths and it was there that John Gay, author
of *The Beggar's Opera*, would sit watching the passers-
by during his visit to Edinburgh in 1732. It was in the
Luckenbooths that Ramsay set up the first circulating library

in Scotland in 1728, a move that aroused some opposition from church circles.

Below Ramsay were the premises of another bookseller and publisher, William Creech (1745–1815). Creech had served on the jury in the trial of Deacon Brodie and in 1811 became Lord Provost, but he is largely remembered now as a literary figure. He wrote for a number of newspapers, and his articles were later collected into a volume *Fugitive Pieces*. He was reknowned for his literary salons at his home in nearby Craig's Close, while his shop was:

> the natural resort of lawyers, authors and all sorts of literary idlers who were always buzzing about the convenient hive. All who wished to see a poet or a stranger or to hear the public news, the last joke by Erskine, or yesterday's occurrence in the Parliament House, or to get the publications of the day, congregated there; lawyers, doctors, clergymen and authors.[24]

Creech published the Edinburgh edition of Burns' poetry and initially their relations were cordial, but the poet soon grew exasperated when Creech held back payment from the sale of his poems.

A favourite haunt of Burns, during his visits to Edinburgh, was Dawney Douglas's Anchor Tavern, which was situated in Anchor Close. This was the home of the Crochallan Fencibles, a celebrated drinking club founded by William Smellie (1740–95), printer and editor of the *Encyclopaedia Britannica*. Its members read like a roll call of the Scottish Enlightenment: Adam Smith, Adam Fergusson, Henry Mackenzie, Hugh Blair, the law lords Hailes and Monboddo. Burns wrote his collection of bawdy lyrics, later published surreptitiously as *The Merry Muses of Caledonia*, for the Crochallans.

Craig's Close, on the north side of the High Street, has always had strong associations with the printing and publishing industries. During the reign of King James VI of Scotland the Scottish printer Andro Hart, best known for his edition of the Bible and *Psalms in Scottish Meter*, lived and carried out his business there.

Anchor Close

Richard Demarco

Daniel Defore (1660–1731) is supposed to have lived in the Close, having been sent to Edinburgh in 1706 to encourage popular support for the Union. Twenty years later he published the third volume of his 'Tour Thro' the whole Island of Great Britain', in which he gives us one of the best contemporary accounts of the city and its inhabitants.

This part of the north side of the High Street, with its warren of narrow alleys, cavernous walls stretching endlessly above one and the lingering smell of urine, has changed little over the last fifty years. While some tenements have been restored as bijou flats, it is still an area of small bars much as Linklater's eponymous hero Magnus Merriman must have known in the 1930s:

> Like a great battlement the north side of the High Street confronted them. From their lower level a long flight of steps led upwards, a narrow passage between black walls whose farther end was invisible, and on whose middle distance a lamp shone dimly. Here and there on the steps, obscurely seen, were vague figures. Under the lamp, with harsh voice and combative gesture, two men were quarrelling. Another, oblivious to them and perhaps to all the world, leaned against the wall with drooping head. From the high remote darkness of the passage came the shrill sound of a woman laughing, and from the tavern whose door the lamp lighted there issued, muffled by the walls, the multifarious sound of talk and argument and rival songs.[25]

Oliver Goldsmith (1730–74), who was in Edinburgh in the cortège of the Duke of Hamilton in 1753, having studied medicine at the University the year before, experienced a more refined element of the capital. He frequented some of the formal dancing assemblies which took place at the Old Town's Halls, in Old Assembly Close, though with apparent little success.

Close to both College Wynd and Old Assembly Close is the Tron Church, which took its name from its proximity to the old public weighing-beam, the Salt Tron. Traditionally the Tron Church has been the spot to see in the New Year and from which the revellers depart first footing, the Scottish practice of visiting friends immediately after midnight on 31 December.[26]

The church was founded in 1637 to house a congregation displaced from St Giles when the latter became an Episcopalian place of worship. In 1824 a fire destroyed much of the southern side of the High Street between Parliament Square and the church including the latter's spire. Lord Cockburn, who watched the fire, gives a dramatic description in *Memorials of His Time*:

> An alarm was given that the Tron Church was on fire. We ran out from the Court, gowned and wigged and saw that it was the steeple, an old Dutch thing composed of wood, iron, and lead, and edged all the way up with bits of ornament. Some of the sparks of the proceeding night had nestled in it, and had at last blown its dry bones into flame. There could not be a more beautiful firework . . .[27]

Robert Fergusson (1750–74), who was born opposite the Tron, in Cap and Feather Close (destroyed when the North Bridge was built), is regarded, arguably, as Edinburgh's greatest poet. In his long poem, 'Auld Reikie', he gives a marvellous picture of life in the city during the mid-eighteenth century ranging from the taverns of the High Street and the legal world to the Leith races and All-Hallows fair.

Educated at the High School, Fergusson became a Divinity student at St Andrews University. The death of his father forced him to abandon his studies and he began work as a clerk, but also began to write in his spare time. He first appeared as a poet with verses in English—correct and rather uninspired—in 1771 in the *Weekly Magazine and Edinburgh Amusement*, but in 'The Daft-Days', which the same periodical published a year later, Fergusson wrote in Scots, imaginatively and amusingly, and over the next two years revitalised the Scots tradition of verse. Prone to bouts of depression, Fergusson was committed to an asylum where he died at the age of twenty-four. He is buried in the Canongate Churchyard.

Though his life was short and his output small, Fergusson had a considerable literary influence, not least on Burns, and

his reputation has continued to grow in this century, particularly among the poets of the Scots Literary Renaissance. Ann
Smith's one act play *A Vision of Angels* was produced to mark
the bicentenary of his death.

Tweeddale Court takes its name from the town mansion of
the Marquess of that name. Daniel Defoe on his tour in 1724
was struck by a 'plantation of lime-trees behind it, the place
not allowing room for a large garden'. It is hard to imagine
now, but later its gardens extended to the Cowgate.

The Court housed for a time the offices of the former
publishers Oliver & Boyd. The headquarters of the Saltire
Society, which campaigns for a greater awareness of Scottish
culture, and the Scottish Poetry Library are also to be found
in the Court.[28]

Beyond Moubray House in the High Street stands the John
Knox House, with its unmistakeable gables and outside stair.
Strictly speaking the house belonged to James Mosman,
Goldsmith to Mary Queen of Scots, but Knox is supposed
to have spent the last few months of his life here in 1572 and
the building must resemble the manse that Knox did live in
nearby.

Knox (1505–72), one of the most important figures of the
Reformation, had lived abroad until 1559, during which
time he spent two years as a slave in a French galley, was
chaplain to Edward VI and spent four years in Frankfurt
and Geneva. He is perhaps best known for his *History
of the Reformation in Scotland* and the pamphlet *First Blast
of the Trumpet against the Monstrous Regiment of Women*.
Knox's influence on the city of his birth has been enormous
and mixed. Edinburgh's rightly justified reputation for the
quantity and quality of its schools rests in part on his legacy.
He believed in the value of education and encouraged local
communities to support the brightest children of the area
through school. At the same time his strong puritanical
views were passed on so even now the city retains a strong
Calvinist tradition, which is reflected in much of its indig-
enous literature.

The stretch from the top of St Mary's Street to Holyrood is
called the Canongate, or more exactly the Canongate of the

Order of St Augustine. Until 1856 this was a separate burgh and a refuge for those in debt.

Running south off the Canongate is St Mary's Street. A plaque at No 26, now a clothes shop, marks the site of Boyd's Inn where Dr Johnson stayed in 1773. Behind it is Chessels Court, recently restored, which for a time housed the Excise Office, where Deacon Brodie attempted his last burglary.

A little further down the Canongate, opposite New Street, is Old Playhouse Close which between 1747 and 1769 was the site of the Playhouse Theatre. A plaque records that it was here that John Home's play *Douglas* was first performed in 1756.

Home (1722–1808) had been born in Leith and educated at Edinburgh University. Captured at the Battle of Falkirk, he was imprisoned in Doune Castle making his escape by a rope made from bedsheets. He then trained as a minister but continued with his efforts to become a playwright. The first performance of *Douglas* proved to be a great success and provoked from a member of the audience the often-quoted cry 'Whaur's yer Wullie Shakespeare noo?' The Church took exception to a minister writing for the stage and Home was forced to resign his ministry. Alexander 'Jupiter' Carlyle (1722–1805), himself a minister, at Inveresk, evokes the furore in his *Autobiography*:

> The play had unbounded success for a great many nights in Edinburgh, and was attended by all of the literati and most of the judges, who, except one or two, had not been in use to attend the theatre. The town in general was in an uproar of exultation that a Scotchman had written a tragedy of the first rate, and that its merit was first submitted to their judgment. There were a few opposers, however, among those who pretended to taste and literature, who endeavoured to cry down the performance in libellous pamphlets and ballads (for they durst not attempt to oppose it in the theatre itself), and they were openly countenanced by Robert Dundas of Arniston, at that time Lord Advocate, and all his minions and expectants. The High-flying set were unanimous against it, as they thought

it a sin for a clergyman to write a play, let it be ever so moral in its tendency.[29]

Douglas was performed in 1757 in London where Home became so friendly with David Garrick that he was twice chosen as his second in two unfought duels. Charles Kean made his début in the role in 1827 and both Sarah Siddons and her brother John Philip Kemble added it to their repertoire.

Douglas is now rarely performed but it is important in any literary history of Edinburgh for it finally broke the taboos surrounding the theatre. Allan Ramsay had opened the first regular theatre in Edinburgh in 1736 in Carrubbers Close but opposition from the Church had forced its closure a year later. After the performance of '*Douglas*' theatres were licensed. It is a sign of changing attitudes that the hearby Netherbow Arts Centre is run by the Church of Scotland.

Further down on the south side is St John's Street, once one of the most aristocratic quarters in Edinburgh. This was where Tobias Smollett stayed, at what is now No 22, with his sister Mrs Telfer in the summer of 1766 while writing *The Expedition of Humphry Clinker*. Perhaps most importantly in giving a picture of the Edinburgh of the day, the book touches on a national identity:

> . . . they are far from being servile imitators of our modes and fashionable vices. All their customs and regulations of public and private economy, of business and diversion, are in their own stile. This remarkably predominates in their looks, their dress, and manner, their music, and even their cookery. Our 'squire declares, that he knows not another people upon earth, so strongly marked with a national character . . .[30]

One writer who more than any other did much to identify and romanticise this sense of being Scottish was Sir Walter Scott, particularly in the Waverley novels. His printer, James Ballantyne, who was based 10 St John Street (now gone), was one of the few people to know the true identity of its anonymous author.

Richard Demarco '92

THE HOUSE OF THE SISTER OF
TOBIAS SMOLLETT

The two of them had been at Kelso Grammar School together and remained friends throughout their lives. James's nephew was to become the novelist R. M. Ballantyne, best known for the adventure story *Coral Island*.

There is also a Burns connection with the street. It was at the Canongate Kilwinning Lodge of Freemasons, which claims the oldest masonic chapel still in use in the world, that he was inducted a member in February 1787, an occasion commemorated in the famous picture by William Stewart Watson.

On the south side of the Canongate is Huntly House Museum, now home of the City Museum, while opposite is the unusual looking Canongate Tolbooth. Next door and set back behind some railings is the Canongate Kirk. Built in 1688 to house the congregation ousted from the nave of Holyrood Abbey by James VII & II when he converted it to a chapel for the Order of the Thistle, it was here that Prince Charles Edward held prisoner captured English officers after the Battle of Prestonpans in 1745.

Among those buried in the churchyard are the economist Adam Smith (1723–90), who lived nearby in Panmure House for the last twelve years of his life; Mrs Agnes M'Lehose, better known as Burns' 'Clarinda'; and George Drummond, six times Lord Provost and the 'father' of the New Town.

On the west side is the grave of Robert Fergusson. One of Burns' first actions on arriving in Edinburgh in the winter of 1786–7 was to arrange for a headstone for the pauper's grave. The simple inscription, which includes four lines by Burns, reads:

Her Lies
ROBERT FERGUSSON POET
Born September 5th 1751 [*sic*]
Died October 16th 1774
No sculptured Marble here nor pompous lay
No storied Urn nor animated Bust
This simple Stone directs Pale Scotia's way
To pour her Sorrows o'er her Poet's Dust.

HER LIES

ROBERT FERGUSON POET
BORN SEPTEMBER 5TH 1751
DIED OCTOBER 16TH 1974

NO SCULPTURED MARBLE HERE NOR POMPOUSLY
NO STORIED URN NOR ANIMATED BUST
THIS SIMPLE STONE DIRECTS PALE SCOTIA
TO POUR HER SORROWS O'ER HER POETS DUST

TO THE MEMORY OF
AGNES MOUAT
SPOUSE TO ROBERT RUTHERFORD
LATE CAPTAIN REGIMENT OF FOOT
THIS MONUMENT WAS

Richard Demarco 92

ROBERT FERGUSON'S GRAVESTONE
CANONGATE CHURCHYARD.

For Burns Fergusson was 'My elder brother in Misfortune/By far my elder brother in the muse'.

Stevenson, who was born exactly a hundred years after Fergusson, also felt a deep attachment to the poet:

> Ah! what bonds we have—born in the same city; both sickly, both pestered, one nearly to madness, one to the madhouse, with a damnatory creed; both seeing the stars and the dawn, and wearing shoe-leather on the same ancient stones, under the same pends, down the same closes . . . You will never know, nor will any man, how deep this feeling is: I believe Fergusson lives in me.[31]

Further down the Canongate is Whitefoord House, now the Scottish Veterans' Residence. This was the town house of an early patron of Burns, Sir John Whitefoord, as well as being the home of the influential philosopher Dugald Stewart (1753–1828) between 1806 and 1812.[32] Stewart was a crucial figure in the Scottish Enlightenment. Though by no means an original thinker he managed to pass on to his students the idea of a liberal culture and his lectures were highly popular. It was Stewart who, after returning from a holiday in Ayrshire where he had met Burns, passed a copy of the Kilmarnock edition of the poems to Henry Mackenzie. The result was the influential review in the *Lounger* which did so much to establish Burns's reputation.

Directly opposite is Queensberry House, now an old people's hospital. Built in 1681 it remained in the Queensberry family between 1686 and 1801. The house is associated with a macabre tale. The eldest son of the Second Duke, who according to Chambers was 'an idiot of the most unhappy sort—rabid and gluttonous, and who early grew to an immense height', was left alone one day with a kitchen hand. He killed the young boy, placed the body on the spit and then ate him.

John Gay (1685–1732), author of 'The Beggar's Opera' stayed there, while private secretary to the Duchess of Queensberry, after his sequel 'Polly' was prohibited in 1729, because some of the members of the government had been satirized in it. A plaque records that Jenny Ha's Change

House, a tavern frequented by John Gay and Allan Ramsay was situated in front of Queensberry House from 1600 to 1857.

Near the foot of the Canongate on the north side is Whitehorse Close which contains, though now reconstructed, the White Horse Inn which figures in Scott's *Waverley*. It was here that Prince Charles Edward's army had their headquarters and which was the starting point for the coaches to London.[33]

The Abbey of Holyrood was founded in 1128 by David I who, according to legend, had a miraculous escape from death here. While out riding he was attacked by a stag. As the king was about to be gored the stag vanished leaving a cross in his hands—the Holy Rood. In thanksgiving for his escape the king ordered the creation of an Abbey on the spot. All that now remains of the original Abbey is the roofless nave of the church.

The Palace of Holyroodhouse is one of the sights of Edinburgh with its distinctive baronial architecture and fairytale setting against the rugged splendour of Arthur's Seat. The present Palace was begun by King James IV at the beginning of the sixteenth century and, after his death at Flodden in 1513, completed by his son James V. Damaged during the English occupation of 1543, and again by fire during Cromwell's occupation in 1650, it was restored to its present state under the direction of Charles II at the end of the seventeenth century.

When John Wesley (1703–91) paid a visit in the 1770s the Palace was but a shadow of its former self. He noted in his journal:

> I took one more walk through Holyroodhouse, the mansion of ancient kings: but how melancholy an appearance does it make now! The stately rooms are dirty as stables: the colours of the tapestry are quite faded; several of the pictures are cut and defaced. The roof of the royal chapel is fallen in; and the bones of James the Fifth, and the once beautiful Lord Darnley, are scattered about like those of sheep or oxen. Such is human greatness![34]

Little seems to have changed by the 1870s when Stevenson was to write:

> The Palace of Holyrood has been left aside in the growth of Edinburgh, and stands grey and silent in a workman's quarter among breweries and gas works. It is a house of many memories. Great people of yore, kings and queens, buffoons and grave ambassadors, played their stately farce for centuries in Holyrood. Wars have been plotted, dancing has lasted deep into the night, murder has been done in its chambers. There Prince Charlie held his phantom levees, and in a very gallant manner[35]

It was at Holyroodhouse that one of the best known episodes in Scottish history took place—the murder in March 1566 of Mary Queen of Scott's secretary Rizzio on the orders of her husband Darnley. The bloodstained spot, where the terrified Italian was stabbed over fifty times, can still be seen in Mary's apartments.

In his story 'The Silver Mirror', Conan Doyle describes a recurring vision of the murder of Rizzio:

> But I saw more to-night. The crouching man was as visible as the lady whose gown he clutched. He is a little swarthy fellow, with a black pointed beard. He has a loose gown of damask trimmed with fur. The prevailing tints of his dress are red. What a fright the fellow is in, to be sure! He cowers and shivers and glares back over his shoulder. There is a small knife in his other hand, but he is far too tremulous and cowed to use it. Fierce faces, bearded and dark, shape themselves out of the mist. There is one terrible creature, a skeleton of a man, with hollow cheeks and eyes sunk in his head. He also has a knife in his hand. On the right of the woman stands a tall man, very young with flaxen hair, his face sullen and dour. The beautiful woman looks up at him in appeal. So does the man on the ground. This youth seems to be the arbiter of their fate. The crouching man draws closer and hides himself in the woman's skirts. The tall youth bends and tries to drag her away from him. So much I saw last night before the mirror cleared. Shall I never know what it leads to and whence it comes? It is not

a mere imagination, of that I am very sure. Somewhere, some time this scene has been acted, and this old mirror has reflected it. But when—where?[36]

To the north of the Palace is a weird little garden pavilion with pyramidal roof, dormer windows and lofty chimneys, known as Queen Mary's Bath. It is said that Mary used to come here to bathe in white wine, in the hope of making herself more attractive.

Running parallel and to the south of the Canongate is Holyrood Road, now a busy road taking traffic to the south of the city. The Cowgate or Soo-Gate (South Gate) begins just beyond St Mary's Street and burrows under the South and George IV bridges. It is a dank, lightless gorge where on both sides the windowless buildings rise to several storeys. Though there has been some restoration, and a few bars and galleries have opened in the area, it still exudes a sinister feeling.

It is difficult to imagine that during the reign of James III the Cowgate was an aristocratic quarter. Writing in the 1860s Alexander Smith noted that if one stood on the South Bridge and looked down:

> instead of a stream, you see the Cowgate, the dirtiest, narrowest, most densely peopled of Edinburgh streets. Admired once by a French ambassador at the court of one of the James, and yet with certain traces of departed splendour, the Cowgate has fallen into the sere and yellow leaf of furniture brokers, second-hand jewellers, and vendors of deleterious alcohol. These second-hand jewellers' shops, the trinkets seen by bleared gaslight, are the most melancholy sights I know. Watches hang there that once ticked comfortably in the fobs of prosperous men, rings that were once placed by happy bridegrooms on the fingers of happy brides, jewels in which lives the sacredness of death-beds. What tragedies, what disruptions of households, what fell pressure of poverty brought them here! . . . Cowgate is the Irish portion of the city. Edinburgh leaps over it with bridges; its inhabitants are morally and geographically the lower orders. They

keep to their own quarters, and seldom come up to the light of day. Many an Edinburgh man has never set his foot in the street; the condition of the inhabitants is as little known to respectable Edinburgh as are the habits of moles, earth-worms, and the mining population.[37]

The Cowgate becomes the Grassmarket where Candle-maker Row and Victoria Street converge. With its restored medieval houses and original cobbles, it makes an attractive scene. Above to one's right the Castle dramatically hovers, the steep sides of the Castle Rock glistening like smoked glass. Gone are the doss houses and slum housing of yesterday, their place taken by antique shops, bistros and boutiques.

At the most easterly end is the West Bow, the site of the Traverse Theatre from 1969 until its removal to purpose-built premises in Cambridge Street in 1992. The Traverse was founded during the 1962 Edinburgh International Festival, when the Cambridge Footlights then including Graham Chapman, John Cleese, Ian Lang and Trevor Nunn, per-suaded a local landlord to lease Kelly's Paradise, a former doss-house and brothel, in James Court. The Theatre offi-cially opened the following January and since its foundation the Traverse has pioneered many new Scottish plays, by among others Stanley Eveling and Stewart Conn, as well as acting as a focus for experimental theatre in Edinburgh.[38]

At the White Hart Inn, an eighteenth century coaching stop, a plaque states 'in the White Hart Inn Robert Burns stayed during his last visit to Edinburgh 1791.' William Wordsworth (1770–1850) is also supposed to have stayed there on his visit, with his sister Dorothy, in September 1803, during which they visited Walter Scott at Lasswade.

A small enclosed garden in the centre of the Grassmarket marks the site on which the city's public gallows stood until 1784. Here, too, was the scene of the famous Porteous riot in September 1736. Earlier that year two smugglers, Wilson and Robertson, were sentenced to death for a petty crime. Many people felt the sentence had been too severe and when Wilson was cut down from the gallows the crowd threw stones at the guard. The Captain of the Guard, John Porteous, responded by firing on the crowd killing eight. Porteous was put on trial, found guilty but then reprieved. The Edinburgh mob, incensed by what they saw as an affront to the city and Scots' Law, stormed the Tolbooth and dragged Porteous out to be hanged.[39]

Violence is also to be found at the junction of Lady Lawson Street and West Port. Here stood Tanner's Close, where the infamous murderers Burke and Hare lived. When in November 1827 an old man died owing his landlord William Hare £4 in rent, Hare persuaded his lodger William Burke to take the old man's body to Robert Knox, the leading anatomy lecturer at the University. They were paid £7 and promised the same rate for further bodies. Realising that a good living could be made in this way the two men selected their victims largely from among the elderly and sick, plied them with drink and then suffocated them. Burke and Hare might have carried on indefinitely but on Hallowe'en 1828 they were arrested and tried for murder. Hare turned King's Evidence and saved himself at the expense of Burke who was hanged, near St Giles.

Knox was vilified for his 'no questions asked' policy, his house attacked and his effigy burnt. A macabre doggerel was coined:

> Down the Close and up the Stair,
> But and ben wi' Burke and Hare.
> Burke's the butcher, Hare's the thief,
> Knox the man that buys the beef.

Shunned by Edinburgh society, including Sir Walter Scott who accused him of 'trading deep in human flesh', unable to secure a University professorship and distraught by the deaths of his wife in childbirth and then his four-year-old son from scarlet fever, he fled south. In 1856 he obtained a job at the Cancer Hospital in Brompton, dying six years later.[40]

R. DeMarco '72   old Quad - Edinburgh University

The Southside and the University

By the middle of the eighteenth century the city was beginning to expand outside the original city walls, first towards the south, and then to the north and the New Town of James Craig and Robert Adam. This expansion was to inaugurate a corresponding development in Scottish life and letters which would come to be called the Scottish Enlightenment.

One of its most important figures rather neatly straddles the period and indeed the geographical development, growing up on this south side but spending most of his life in the New Town. Walter Scott (1771–1832) was born in what is now Guthrie Street, and was then College Wynd. His father was a lawyer, his mother, Anne Rutherford, the daughter of a former Professor of Medicine at the University. Anne Rutherford had lost her first six children in infancy and this combined with the fact that young Walter was stricken by poliomyelitis, an illness which left him with a permanent limp in his right leg, persuaded the family to move to the nearby George Square, which was regarded as healthier.

George Square was the first development of size outside the old city wall, pre-dating the New Town by some twenty years, and attracted the cream of Edinburgh society. Walter Scott's parents moved to No 25, on the west side, in 1772 where their neighbours included Henry Mackenzie and Lord Braxfield. It was from George Square that Scott went to the High School and to Edinburgh University and it was there that Scott began his literary career with the translation of Burger's 'Lenore'.[41]

Yet another writer associated with George Square is Rebecca West (1892–1983). Born Cicily Isabel Fairfield she was brought up in Edinburgh, attending George Watsons Ladies' College then at 5 George Square, which she called John

Thompson's Ladies' College in her novel *The Judge*. West felt trapped in Edinburgh and the book satirizes the provincial nature of the place:

> They were passing down the Meadow Walk now, between trees that were like shapes drawn on blotting-paper and lamps that had the smallest scope.
>
> 'Edinburgh's a fine place,' he said. 'It can handle even an asphalt track with dignity.'
>
> 'Oh, a fine place,' she answered pettishly, 'if you could get away from it.'[42]

West left the city of her youth as a young woman never to return, and her reputation is based largely on books like *The Return of the Soldier* and *The Meaning of Treason*.

The University of Edinburgh now dominates George Square. Against much opposition most of the square was pulled down in the 1960s to build the huge David Hume and William Robertson towers on the east side and the library, designed by Basil Spence, on the south side. Only the west side and the gardens have survived.

Robert Garioch (1909–81), a graduate of the university and one of the most distinguished twentieth-century Edinburgh writers, in his poem 'A Wee Local Scandal' gives some indication of the passions unleashed over the episode:

> The University has got a wee
> skyscraper at the corner of George Square,
> fowerteen storeys, the day I wes there;
> it's maybe sunk; I've no been back to see –
>
> the Hume Toure—it hits ye in the ee,
> yon muckle black rectangle in the air,
> a graund sicht frae the Meedies, man; it fair
> obliterates Arthur's Seat, nae word of a lee.
>
> But whit a scandal. That's the Dauvit Hume
> plewed in the professorial election;
> hou can the outwail'd candidate presume
>
> to name sic architectural perfection?
> Dauvit Hume Toure, indeed. Whit a let-doun.
> It shuid hae been the Will Cleghorn Erection.

Garioch was a schoolmaster in the city all his life apart from the Second World War, much of which he spent in Italian and German POW camps, an experience from which he never properly recovered.

Edinburgh has provided much of the inspiration for Garioch's work, much as it did for his hero Robert Fergusson, though he remains by no means uncritical of the city of his birth. In 'To Robert Fergusson' he looks back with some regret to the Edinburgh of the eighteenth century:

> Auld Reekie's bigger, nou, what's mair,
> and folk hae the greater share
> of warldlie gear may tak the air
> in Morningside,
> and needna sclim the turnpike stair
> whar ye wad byde.

> But truth it is, our couthie city
> has cruddit in twa pairts a bittie
> and speaks twa tongues, ane coorse and grittie,
> heard in the Cougait
> the tither copied, mair's the pitie,
> frae Wast of Newgate.

Garioch's *Collected Poems* was published in 1977 and, after slow recognition, he has come to be regarded as one of Scotland's finest twentieth-century poets. He is comemmorated by a plaque, placed in 1983 by the Saltire Society, at 4 Nelson Street.[43]

Buccleuch Place, a wide street of tall but rather stony-faced houses, now occupied by university departments, lies immediately behind the David Hume Tower. Built in the 1780s it was almost as fashionable as George Square. Lord Cockburn looking back from the vantage point of the 1820s remembered how:

> in Buccleuch Place (close by the south-eastern corner of the square) most beautiful rooms were erected, which, for several years, threw the New Town piece of presumption entirely into the shade. . . . Here were the last remains of the ball-room disciplines of the preceeding generation.

Martinet dowagers and venerable beaux acted as masters and mistresses of ceremonies, and made all the preliminary arrangements. No couple could dance unless each party was provided with a ticket prescribing the precise place in the precise dance. If there was no ticket, the gentleman, or the lady, was dealt with as an intruder, and turned out of the dance. If the ticket had marked upon it—say for a country dance, the figures 3.5; this meant that the holder was to place himself in the third dance, and fifth from the top; and if he was anywhere else, he was set right or excluded. And the partner's ticket must correspond. Woe on the poor girl who with ticket 2.7, was found opposite a youth marked 5.9![44]

Further down Buccleuch Place at No 18, now part of the Sociology and Scandinavian departments, lived Francis Jeffrey (1773–1850) in a house that has now entered Edinburgh literary history. It was there in March 1802 that the *Edinburgh Review* was founded. Over the next twenty years the magazine would become so influential that it drew writers from all over Britain, turning Edinburgh into the literary capital of the land. Part of its success was due to its editor, Jeffrey, and part due to the support of its publisher Archibald Constable, who paid the contributors to the magazine very generously. Walter Scott was a contributor until 1808, when, appalled by the magazine's Whig sympathies, he became involved in the founding of the Tory *Quarterly Review*.

Across the Meadows, in a rather anonymous and run-down part of the city, is Sciennes Hill House. The two-storey house, built of rough stone has now been divided into flats and forms part of Sciennes House Place, a small street running west off Causewayside.

A small plaque on the wall commemorates the famous meeting between the sixteen-year-old Walter Scott and Robert Burns in 1787, at the home of the Professor of Moral Philosophy, Adam Ferguson. A vivid account of the meeting and description of Burns is given in Lockhart's *Life of Sir Walter Scott*:

His person was strong and robust; his manners rustic,

SCIENNES HILL HOUSE   Richard Demarco '92

not clownish; a sort of dignified plainness and simplicity, which received part of its effect perhaps from one's knowledge of his extraordinary talents . . . There was a strong expression of sense and shrewdness in all his lineaments; the eye alone, I think, indicated the poetical character and temperament. It was large and of a dark cast, and glowed (I say literally glowed) when he spoke with feeling or interest.[45]

A good idea of what the house looked like can be gained by turning north round the corner and looking over the wall.

Towards the end of his life Thomas De Quincey (1785–1859) lodged at 42 Lothian Street, now swept away by the Edinburgh University Student Centre. He had come to Edinburgh from the Lake District in 1820, and was to spend the next forty years of his life in a series of addresses around the city.[46]

The demands of a large family and a limited income from his writing for Blackwoods meant that for much of that time he seemed to be dodging creditors, even though the publication of *Confessions of an English Opium Eater* in 1821 immediately established him in the first rank of writers. He is buried in St Cuthbert's churchyard at the west end of Princes Street.

Lothian Street runs into Potterrow in which Burns's 'Clarinda' lived. Burns had met Agnes M'Lehose in December 1787 on his second visit to Edinburgh. At the time she was in her late twenties and a grass widow with three small children. Her husband James, a law agent, had married her when she was a teenager, against her father's wishes, and then fled to Jamaica to escape his debtors. Attracted perhaps as much by Burns's reputation as a lover, as his talents as a poet, she invited him to have tea with her. Though unable to attend, Burns wrote to her and so began the correspondence between 'Sylvander' and 'Clarinda'.[47]

The affair between the 'ploughman poet' and the 'lady of fashion' soon became public knowledge and only ended when Burns left Edinburgh. It has left us with one of Burns's finest poems *Ae Fond Kiss*:

Fare-thee-weel, thou first and fairest!
Fare-thee-weel, thou best and dearest!
Thine be ilka joy and treasure,
Peace, Enjoyment, Love and Pleasure!

Ae fond kiss, and then we sever!
Ae fareweel, Alas for ever!
Deep in heart-wrung tears I'll pledge thee,
Warring sighs and groans I'll wage thee.

They in fact met once more, just before she left for Jamaica in the hope of affecting a reconciliation with her husband. A pathetic entry in her diary for 6th December 1831 shows she loved him 'till the shadow fell'. 'This day I can never forget. Parted with Robert Burns in the year 1791 never more to meet in this world. Oh may we meet in heaven.' She died aged eighty two in a tenement flat in the lower Calton on 22nd October 1841, having survived Burns by forty five years.

One of Edinburgh's best known churches is Greyfriars Kirk at the top of Candlemaker Row. Originally a convent established by Dutch friars in the thirteenth century the kirk was opened in 1620, the first new church to be built in Edinburgh since the Reformation. Stevenson described it as:

> one of our famous Edinburgh points of view; and strangers are led thither to see, by yet another instance, how strangely the city lies upon her hills. The enclosure is of an irregular shape; the double church of Old and New Greyfriars stands on the level at the top; a few thorns are dotted here and there, and the ground falls by terrace and steep slope towards the north. The open shows many slabs and table tombstones; and all round the margin the place is girt by an array of aristocratic mausoleums appallingly adorned.[48]

Little seems to have changed in the century since he wrote those lines. There is a sense of calm about the place, a feeling that the quiet graves are watching one and have some tales to tell.

The church is best known for its associations with the

Covenanters. This was a movement that grew up in opposition to Charles I's proclamation that the Episcopal faith would
be Scotland's religion. It was in the southern annexe of the
Churchyard that the 1200 Covenanting prisoners were held
because the prisons were full and here that the Covenant was
signed in 1638 on the through-stane or horizontal gravestone
on the south side of the church. Near the steps leading to
the northern entrance is the Martyrs' Monument.

The graveyard has been called the Westminster Abbey of
Edinburgh. Among the important literary figures buried in
the churchyard are the unfortunate Captain Porteous; George
Buchanan, tutor to Mary Queen of Scots and her son James
as well as the author of an important history of Scotland; William Creech; Sir George Mackenzie of Rosehaugh,
founder of the Advocates' Library; Clement Little, founder
of the University Library; and the poet Allan Ramsay.

A plain mural tablet on the north side of the terrace
commemorates Henry Mackenzie (1745–1831), an important
linking figure between the Edinburgh of Fergusson and that
of Burns. Born on the day Bonnie Prince Charlie landed
in 1745, Mackenzie had several addresses in the city, most
notably 6 Heriot Row, where he died. At one stage he was
the most popular British novelist of his generation, though
his most famous book *A Man of Feeling* (1771) now seems
weak and sentimental. Scott dedicated *Waverley* to 'Our
Scottish Addison, Henry Mackenzie'. During his lifetime
he was highly thought of as an essayist but his posthumous
reputation rests principally on his championing of Byron,
Burns and Scott.[49]

Also buried in Greyfriars is the Gaelic poet Duncan Ban
MacIntyre (1724–1812). Though best known for his long
poem 'Praise of Ben Dorain' he was also a shrewd commentator on the growing divisions between the social classes in
Edinburgh. MacIntyre spent over half his life in Edinburgh,
and though largely unknown in his own lifetime was an inspiration to subsequent poets such as Hugh MacDiarmid.

Greyfriars church, which figures in *Guy Mannering*, has
many associations with Sir Walter Scott. His father is buried
there and it was while coming out of the church that the
teenage Walter first met a fifteen-year old girl, who many

think to have been the love of his life. She was the daughter of Sir John and Lady Jane Stuart-Belsches and was not only well born but also an heiress. His attentions came to nothing and a few years later she married a friend of his called William Forbes.[50]

Scott was heartbroken and even thirty years later wondered why it 'should still agitate my heart'. Williamina Stuart-Belsches is often thought to have been the model for Greenmantle in *Redgauntlet* and Margaret in *The Lay of the Last Minstrel*. She died in 1810 at the age of thirty-five.

In 1797, while in the Lake District, Scott met a French *émigrée* Charlotte Carpentier to whom he immediately proposed marriage. There is some suggestion this could have been on the rebound from Williamina, who had married shortly before, and certainly he was to write:

> Mrs Scott's match and mine was of our own making and proceeded from the most sincere affection on both sides, which has rather increased than diminished during twelve years' marriage. But it was something short of love in all its forms, which I suspect people only feel once in all their lives; folk who have been nearly drowned in bathing rarely venturing a second time out of their depth.[51]

George Heriot's School, next door to Greyfriars, is mentioned in Scott's novel *The Fortunes of Nigel*. Founded by a wealthy goldsmith in the seventeenth century it has educated many eminent writers, including, in this century, the historical novelist Nigel Tranter (1909–   ). Edward Topham on his visit to Edinburgh in 1774 thought that it was 'a large and magnificent edifice, and has infinitely more the look of a palace than Holyroodhouse'—a characteristic it shares with many of Edinburgh's schools. The novel *Walter Crighton or Reminiscences of George Heriot's Hospital* (1898) by Jamieson Baillie-Livingston gives a good idea of the nineteenth century schoolboy's experiences there.

Education has always been highly valued in the city and nowhere more so than the University of Edinburgh, the original part of which is situated at the eastern end of Chambers Street. Founded in 1582 as the 'Tounis College', the university buildings stood on the site of Kirk o' Field, the house which was blown up in 1567 causing the death of Mary Queen of Scot's husband, Lord Darnley. Mary shortly afterwards married the Earl of Bothwell and it was Mary's perceived involvement in the murder which ended her honeymoon period with the Scottish people. A number of novels have commemorated this well-known episode in Scottish history.

The University quickly flourished and was at the fore-front of the Scottish Enlightenment. Matthew Bramble, the central character of Tobias Smollett's novel *The Expedition of Humphry Clinker*, noted that:

> Edinburgh is a hot-bed of genius. I have had the good fortune to be made acquainted with many authors of the first distinction: such as the two Humes, Robertson, Smith, Wallace, Blair, Fergusson, Wilkie etc, and I have found them all as agreeable in conversation as they are instructive and entertaining in their writings.[52]

Of the above names almost all had either been educated or taught at the University. They included David Hume, the historian and philosopher; John Home, the dramatist; William Robertson, the historian and Principal of the University; Adam Smith, author of *The Wealth of Nations* and Adam Ferguson, who, with his *Essay on the History of Civil Society*, founded the modern discipline of sociology. These men were to create an 'Athens of the North' and in turn to attract writers and scholars to the city.

Walter Scott spent several years at the University in the 1780s studying for the general arts degree, but was forced to leave early through ill health. In the next century Charles Darwin spent two years at the University from 1825, lodging in nearby Lothian Street. He complained of finding the lectures dull and spent much of his time collecting specimens from the Forth.

The present buildings were erected between 1789 and 1834, with the dome added in 1887. Though much of the University has now decamped to George Square some of the University administration is still situated there.

Thomas Carlyle (1795–1881) arrived at the University in November 1809, after a three-day walk from his birthplace of Ecclefechan in Dumfries. His first lodgings were in Simon Square, now reached through Gibb's Entry and later he moved to Bristo Street. He quickly threw himself into his studies for a general arts degree, distinguishing himself in both Latin and Mathematics.

In 1817, after teaching in Annan and Kirkcaldy, he took a new direction and returned to Edinburgh to start his theological training and also began to write. It was a time of great personal unhappiness, partly because of his dislike of his subject and teachers and partly just loneliness. He was to remain in Edinburgh for another eleven years lodging in the New Town, off Leith Walk and at 21 Comely Bank, then with views over green fields, where he spent eighteen months immediately after his marriage in 1826. In 1828 he left to seek his fame and fortune in London having failed in his application for the Chair of English Literature. However Edinburgh remained dear to his heart and he returned as Rector of the University in 1866, an honour he regarded as the greatest of his life. Now eminent as a historian, social writer and thinker his speech, in which he reviewed his time at the University, was a success but his joy was mitigated by the death of his wife three weeks later. Inheriting her estate of Craigenputtock he donated it, together with ten bursaries, to the University. Herr Teufelsdrörckh's university in the autobiographical *Sartor Resartus* is based on Edinburgh.

It is strange to imagine that three writers—Robert Louis Stevenson (1850–94), J. M. Barrie (1860–1937) and Arthur Conan Doyle (1859–1930)—attended the University within the space of a few years.

Stevenson greatly admired Barrie's work and repeatedly invited him to Vailima. He wrote to Henry James in December 1892 'You and Barrie and Kipling are my Muses Three' while to Barrie he went further

I am proud to think you are a Scotchman . . . and please do not think when I thus seem to bracket myself with you, that I am wholly blinded with vanity . . . I am a capable artist; but it begins to look to me as if you are a man of genius.[53]

Stevenson seems to have been drawn by the fact that 'both made our stages in the metropolis of the minds: our Virgil's "grey metropolis" and I count that a lasting bond.'

Barrie includes a portrait of Stevenson in his reminiscences of the University, *An Edinburgh Eleven*, and on Stevenson's death wrote an elegiac poem 'Scotland's Lament'.

Conan Doyle also had a great deal of respect for Stevenson. He was asked to finish *St Ives* but 'did not feel equal to the task'. It was done by Arthur Quiller-Couch instead. Towards the end of his life Stevenson began a correspondence with Conan Doyle in which he professed his admiration for the Sherlock Holmes stories.

In turn Barrie and Conan Doyle were friends. In 1893 they collaborated on an English comic opera *Jane Annie* but it was not a success. Conan Doyle in his autobiography claimed it 'was a bitter thought for both of us' but it does not seem to have affected their friendship.

Stevenson spent several unhappy years at the University between 1867 and 1875, where he cared little for his studies. He rarely attended his engineering classes, preferring to spend his time walking, talking and drinking. His time at University was mitigated only by the chance to edit the University magazine and by his membership of the Speculative Society.

'The Spec', which still exists, was the University literary & debating society. Founded in 1764, it has traditionally been dominated by lawyers and writers. Stevenson was twice President of the Society and wrote several papers for it.[54] The weekly meetings in Stevenson's time were from eight to midnight, but were broken at nine when some of the members would leave 'to buy pencils'. This was in fact to go for a drink at Rutherford's Bar in nearby Drummond Street. Twenty years after his visits Stevenson was to write to his old friend, Charles Baxter:

> Last night as I lay under my blanket . . . all of a sudden I had a vision of—Drummond Street. It came on me like a flash of lightning: I simply returned thither, and into the

past. And when I remember all I hoped and feared as I pickled about Rutherford's in the rain and the east wind; how I feared I should make a mere shipwreck, and yet timidly hoped not; how I feared I should never have a friend, far less a wife, and yet passionately hoped I might; how I hoped (if I did not take to drink) I should possibly write one little book etc. etc. And then now—what a change! I feel somehow as if I should like the incident set upon a brass plate at the corner of that dreary thoroughfare for all students to read, poor devils, when their hearts are down.[55]

J.M. Barrie matriculated in 1878 at the age of eighteen. His intention after leaving Dumfries Academy had been to become a writer immediately, but his mother persuaded him that he should first obtain a university education. A fellow student Robert Galloway later remembered Barrie as:

> a sallow-faced, round-shouldered, slight, somewhat delicate-looking figure, who quietly went in and out amongst us, attracting but little observation, but himself observing all and measuring up men and treasuring up impressions.[56]

Barrie lodged first in a top floor flat at 14 Cumberland Street and later at 20 Shandwick Place. He leaves a picture of his contemporaries and teachers in *An Edinburgh Eleven*. On graduating Barrie took lodgings at 3 Great King Street, with a Mrs Edwards who was to provide the inspiration for his story 'The Old Lady Shows Her Medals'. Shortly afterwards he was offered a job as a leader writer on the *Nottingham Journal* and never again lived in Edinburgh. However he did return to receive an honorary LL.D. in 1909 and as Chancellor of the University in 1930, when he succeeded Lord Balfour who had been Chancellor for forty years. Perhaps this later recognition persuaded him to look upon his Alma Mater rather more generously for he left £5,000 to it in his will.

S. R. Crockett, whose name was to be so commonly linked with Barrie as a member of the Kailyard School, was in the last year of his Arts course at the University when Barrie matriculated, though they do not seem to have met. Crockett though the same age as Barrie had gone up aged fifteen. He later returned to study theology at the New Theological College but after Barrie had left.

Crockett, a Free Church minister until able to become a full time author, wrote over forty novels, of which the best known *The Stickit Minister* is dedicated to R. L. Stevenson. In turn Stevenson dedicated his 'Hills of Home' poem to Crockett. In his novel *Cleg Kelly, Arab of the City*, Crockett drew from his experiences as a missionary in the Edinburgh slums and the book has many scenes around the St Leonards area of the city where he lodged as a student.

Arthur Conan Doyle began his medical studies in 1876, graduating as a Bachelor of Medicine in 1881 and going on to take his doctorate on aspects of syphilis in 1885. As a student he lodged in Howe Street in the New Town.

In his semi-autobiographical and largely forgotten early novel *The Firm of Girdlestone* he leaves a bitter picture of the university:

> Edinburgh University may call herself, with grim jocose-ness, the 'alma mater' of her students, but if she be a mother at all, she is one of a very stoic and spartan cast, who conceals her maternal affections with remarkable success. The only signs of interest she ever deigns to evince towards her alumni are upon those not infrequent occasions when guineas are to be demanded from them . . . The University is a great unsympathetic machine, taking in a stream of raw-boned cartilaginous youths at one end, and turning them out at the other as learned divines, astute lawyers and skilful medical men. Of every thousand of the raw material about six hundred emerge at the other side. The remainder are broken in the process.[57]

Conan Doyle was perhaps being rather unfair. The University was cosmopolitan with a large intake from England and the colonies. It was while he was at Edinburgh that his first story was published. 'The Mystery of Sasassa Valley', a light-hearted thriller set in South Africa about a demon who turned out to be a diamond, appeared in *Chambers' Journal* in September 1879. Conan Doyle's literary career had begun.

SANDY BELL's AT FORRESTHILL   Richard Demarco '92

At the University Conan Doyle met a man who was to change his life: Joseph Bell (1837–1911), a lecturer and surgeon at the Royal Infirmary of Edinburgh:

> Bell was a very remarkable man in body and mind. He was thin, wiry, dark, with a high-nosed acute face, penetrating grey eyes, angular shoulders, and a jerky way of walking. His voice was high and discordant. He was a very skilful surgeon, but his strong point was diagnosis, not only of disease, but of occupation and character.[58]

Conan Doyle became his clerk responsible for preparing case notes and showing patients into 'the large room in which Bell sat in state surrounded by his dressers and students'. This allowed him to observe the doctor's extraordinary powers of deduction. It was on Bell that Conan Doyle later modelled his detective Sherlock Holmes.

Pupil and master stayed in touched and Bell took a keen interest in the Sherlock Holmes stories 'and even made suggestions which were not', Doyle noted, 'very practical'. Bell cleverly managed to profit from the association by contributing a Preface for *A Study in Scarlet*, a book for which Conan Doyle was paid £25 for the copyright.

The Forresthill Bar, better known as Sandy Bell's, in Forrest Road, famous as a venue for folk music, had a number of literary associations most notably with the writers Stuart MacGregor and Hamish Henderson. Henderson (1919–) is best known as a folklorist and the founder of the School of Scottish Studies at Edinburgh University, where he has taught since 1951, though he first made his reputation as a poet with *Elegies for the dead in Cyrenaica* (1948), based on his experiences during the Desert War, and since then as a translator of Gramsci's *Prison Letters*. His poem *Floret silva undique* from the sequence *Auld Reekie's Roses* gives a picture of an Edinburgh freed from its Calvinist tradition.

Almost opposite the Old Buildings of the University is Infirmary Street, and at the foot in High School Yards is the old High School of Edinburgh. Though the peripatetic school is thought to be over 800 years old, it was not until the sixteenth century that much is known about it.

THE old High School   Richard Demarco '92

Its former pupils include the poet William Drummond of Hawthornden (1585–1649), the founder of the New Town George Drummond, Robert Fergusson, and more recently Sydney Goodsir Smith, Norman MacCaig and Karl Miller.

Walter Scott began there in 1779 two years after it opened in the new building, recollecting that he 'glanced like a meteor from one end of the class to the other, and commonly disgusted my kind master as much by negligence and frivolity as I occasionally pleased him by flashes of intellect and talent'.

He was followed shortly afterwards by Henry Cockburn who leaves in *Memorials of His Time* a vivid description of the 'usual High School apparel':

> It consisted of a round black hat; a shirt fastened at the neck by a black ribbon, and except on dress days, unruffled; a cloth waistcoat, rather large, with two rows of buttons and of buttonholes, so that it could be buttoned on either side, which, when one side got dirty, was convenient; a singlebreasted jacket, which in due time got a tail and became a coat; brown corduroy breeches, tied at the knees by a showy knot of brown cotton tape; worsted stockings in winter, blue cotton stockings in summer, and white cotton for dress; clumsy shoes made to be used on either foot, and each requiring to be used on alternate feet daily; brass or copper buckles. The coat and waistcoat were always of glaring colours, such as bright blue, grass green, and scarlet. I remember well the pride with which I was once rigged out in a scarlet waistcoat and a bright green coat. No such machinery as what are now termed braces or suspenders had then been imagined.[59]

If one carries on down the South Bridge and crosses the High Street one comes, after *The Scotsman* office, to the North Bridge. The present North Bridge dates from the end of the last century, though its predecessor, built in the 1760s, was the first part of the New Town expansion.

Edward Topham, visiting Edinburgh fourteen years later, was immediately struck by the strong winds on the bridge, a situation which has not changed to this day. If one can withstand the wind the North Bridge is a marvellous vantage point to look out on Edinburgh. S.R. Crockett has a powerful description in his novel *Kit Kennedy* of the view from the bridge with Waverley Station 'sunk in a pale, luminous, silver mist through which burnt a thousand lights, warm, yellow and kindly', while Stevenson used to lean on the parapet of the bridge and watch the trains departing.

> on a voyage to brighter skies. Happy the passengers who shake off the dust of Edinburgh, and have heard for the last time the cry of the east wind among her chimney tops! And yet the place establishes an interest in people's hearts; go where they will, they take a pride in their old home.[60]

WATERLOO

TLAND

FORTE
BARMORAL HOTEL AND CLOCKTOWER

WEST END   25
MAYFIELD   26
MEADOWBANK

Richard Demarco

The New Town

The Old Town had become so overcrowded by the mid-eighteenth century that expansion was required. Some 25,000 people were crammed into 138 acres. It was George Drummond, six times Lord Provost, whose ideas were embodied in the 1752 *Proposals*. Between 1763 and 1772 the North Bridge was built across the Nor Loch to link up with Edinburgh's port of Leith, and in 1766 a competition was announced for designs for a New Town.

A twenty-seven-year-old architect James Craig won the competition using one of the oldest of town planning patterns: the chequerboard or gridiron. His scheme involved a wide central street on the crest of the hill which he named after the ruling monarch George. This was balanced by two open-sided terraces: Princes Street and Queen Street. Between them ran two smaller streets, Thistle and Rose streets, designed to accommodate coach houses, shops and tradesmen's homes. At each end of George Street there was to be a church: St Andrew's at the east and St George's at the west; the Act of Union still within living memory, the intention was to show the partnership of Scotland and England.

Soon the wealthy flocked north to the healthier and less crowded climes of this new development and the New Town was born.

There has, however, always been an awkward division between the Old Edinburgh and the New Town. It is Princes Street that marks the dividing line between the medieval town with its buildings etched haphazardly against the skyline and the ordered symmetry of the New Town. To the south the turrets, crowstepped gables, chimneys and spires of the High Street, to the north the fanlights, delicately scrolled lampholders and brass doorplates of George Street and Heriot Row.

Eric Linklater well recognised this demarcation line when he described Princes Street as 'a sort of schizophrenia in stone'.[61] Princes Street has always been the preserve of the commercial world and is now dominated by the household names to be found in most High Streets in the country. Khalid, the central character of Joan Lingard's *The Prevailing Wind*, is scathing about it:

> Let us contemplate the streets of the Princes, the home of the shortbread kings and the Baronets of Bombazine. It is a fine street, is it not, despite its vulgar moments? It has width and colour, gardens and a bandstand, a gallery of art with another tucked behind, and a big ugly hotel at either end. What more could a street want.[62]

The two hotels, he refers to, are the Balmoral (formerly the North British) at the east end and the Caledonian at the west. Muriel Spark stayed for several weeks at the North British during her father's final illness.

> I spent most of my time in my room waiting for the hours of visiting my father to come round. I think at such times in one's life one tends to look out of the window oftener and longer than usual. I left my work and my books and spent my time at the window. It was a high, wide window, with an inside ledge, broad and long enough for me to sit in comfortably with my legs stretched out. The days before Easter were suddenly warm and sunny. From where I sat propped in the open window frame, I could look straight onto Arthur's Seat and the Salisbury Crags, its girdle. When I sat the other way round I could see part of the Old City, the east corner of Princes Street Gardens, and the black Castle Rock. In those days I experienced an inpouring of love for the place of my birth, which I am aware was psychologically connected with my love for my father and with the exiled sensation of occupying a hotel room which was really meant for strangers.[63]

Opposite the Balmoral is West Register Street and the site of Ambrose's, a tavern which became the centre of a satire

on Edinburgh life which ran in *Blackwood's Magazine* between
1822 and 1835. So famous did it become that it was itself
satirised in *Peter's Letters to his Kinsfolk*.[64]

Written by James Hogg and John Wilson the *Noctes
Ambrosianae* were a series of topical, critical, political and
convivial dialogues that were supposed to have taken place
in Ambrose's tavern and described the activities of, among
others, the 'Ettrick Shepherd', 'Christopher North' and the
'Opium Eater', characters based respectively on James Hogg,
John Wilson and Thomas De Quincey.

James Hogg (1770–1835) was born and brought up as a
shepherd in the Borders, but is now best remembered for
his third novel, *The Confessions of a Justified Sinner*, which
has several vivid scenes set in Edinburgh, such as the duel
in the High Street and the scene in which Robert Wringhim
tries to push his mother off Arthur's Seat. Published in 1824,
it is considered one of the most profound novels ever written
about Calvinism.[65]

The first house to be built in Princes Street was in 1769 at
No 10, on the site now opposite the Balmoral Hotel. Here
Archibald Constable (1774–1815) set up his publishing firm
in 1822 and here his authors Scott, Lockhart, Jeffrey and
Cockburn would meet.[66]

Constable was an important catalyst in the establishing
of Edinburgh as a literary centre. Cockburn wrote of his
publisher:

> Abandoning the old timid and grudging system, Constable
> stood out as the general patron of all promising publica-
> tions, and confounded not merely his rivals in trade, but his
> very authors, by his unheard-of prices. Ten, even twenty,
> guineas for a sheet of a review, £2,000 or £3,000 for a single
> poem, and £1,000 each for two philosophical dissertations,
> drew authors from dens where they would otherwise have
> starved, and made Edinburgh a literary mart, famous with
> strangers, and the pride of its own citizens.[67]

A few doors west at No 17 another bookseller William
Blackwood (1776–1834) had been established for some six
years, after moving from his premises at 64 South Bridge.

Blackwood had entered the bookselling trade in 1790 and by the time he was established in Princes Street was a wealthy man. For example just before moving he had published Walter Scott's *Tales of My Landlord*, which had sold 6,000 copies in a week.[68]

In 1817 Blackwood founded the magazine, that was to take his name, determined to provide a rival to the Whig *Edinburgh Review*. He astutely 'made an arrangement with a gentleman of first-rate talents by which I will begin a new work of a far superior kind'. The gentleman was John Wilson (1785–1854), already encountered as the co-author of the *Noctes Ambrosianae*. After Oxford, where he had been the first winner of the Newdigate Prize for Poetry, Wilson travelled widely throughout Britain, sometimes disguised as a tinker. He spent seven years in the Lake District, where he was friendly with De Quincey and Wordsworth, and then after losing most of his fortune came to Edinburgh in 1814, to complete his law studies. He had a variety of addresses around the New Town.[69]

The other editor, J. G. Lockhart (1794–1854) had been educated at Glasgow and Oxford, and at the time *Blackwood's* was launched was only twenty-three. A striking man with his well-shaped head and piercing eyes, he was also rather deaf which led people to assume he was aloof. Between 1837 and 1838 he published a seven-volume life of his father-in-law, Sir Walter Scott.

It was an article that appeared in the October 1817 issue that overnight was to put *Blackwood's* firmly on the literary map. The Chaldee Manuscript was a satirical portrait of the literary and political figures of the day, written in the language of the Old Testament. The Whigs and their supporters were lampooned, the Tories praised, and though now the contents look dated and parochial, at the time it attracted attention all over the country.

Suddenly the magazine had found a voice, which increasingly became vituperative. Its reputation and sales were consolidated by the success of the *Noctes Ambrosianae* and the ten-year association with Thomas De Quincey. In 1830 it moved to 45 George Street where a future contributor would be Sir Walter Scott.

It is Scott who in more ways than one dominates Edinburgh. Towering over Princes Street is perhaps the most famous literary association, and certainly the largest memorial in the city. Completed in 1844 at a cost of some £15,000 the Scott Monument (intended originally to be sited in Charlotte Square) was the work of a young self-taught architect George Meikle Kemp, who was found drowned in the Union Canal, necessitating the work to be completed by his brother-in-law, William Bonnar.

The monument takes the form of an open Gothic cross surmounted by an ornately detailed spire rising to 200 ft. The statue in grey Carrara marble cut by John Steell depicts the seated Scott wrapped in a shepherd's plaid with his deerhound Maida at his feet. The exterior is decorated by eighty-four statuettes of characters from his novels and figures from Scottish history; the four most prominent, above the main arches, being Prince Charles Edward, the Lady of the Lake, Meg Merrilees and the Last Minstrel.

The Mound was formed from the earth thrown out when digging the foundations of the streets in the New Town. Begun in 1781 it had by 1830 assumed its present dimensions. When work was at its height more than 1,800 cartloads of rubble were being deposited each day. At the time Henry Cockburn described it as an 'abominable incumbrance' but it forms a useful link between the Old and New Towns and is now totally identified with Edinburgh.

Some of the best views of Princes Street are from the top of the Mound. Alexander Cross in James Allan Ford's novel *A Statue for a Public Place* looks down to:

> the bottom of the Mound, the National Gallery of Scotland with its Ionic columns and the gallery of the Royal Scottish Academy with its Doric columns, and on either side of them the valley with trees in cold-burnt leaf and flower-beds in cinderglow, and along the opposite brink of the valley the mile-straight stretch of Princes Street, concealing behind its architectural confusion the eighteenth-century classical grace of the New Town. He saw it all with

disturbing clarity, the familiar revealed as unfamiliar. He saw it all and was excited by it and felt obliged to explain his excitement. There was no magic in the unfamiliarity, nothing that had dropped out of God's sleeve. It was caused by the slant of the sun and by the unusual stillness and dryness of the air: this October light, making a long thrust from the south-east, had a cold-tempered point that whittled every outline against the sky, laid bare every sunward surface, sliced off clean shadows and cut out a deep perspective; this northern air had its own power of refraction and, indeed, its own power of heady stimulation.[70]

Joyce Cary (1888–1957), used to have classes in the Royal Scottish Academy, then the Royal Institute Building while studying at the Board of Manufacturers School of Art, now the Edinburgh College of Art between 1907 and 1909. While in Edinburgh Cary lodged with a Miss Yule at 16 St Bernards Crescent. It was in Edinburgh that Cary abandoned painting for writing and where his first book, a collection of poetry, was published. Cary was to look back fondly to his time in Edinburgh and would later receive an honorary Doctorate of Laws from the University. It was while returning on the train from a lecture in Edinburgh in 1942 that Cary began his best known novel, *The Horse's Mouth*.

Edinburgh is famous for its bitter wind and no where is it more apparent than Princes Street. Magnus in Eric Linklater's *Magnus Merriman* suffers its full force:

The wind hurried him along Princes Street. It blew with a bellow and a buffet on his stern and half-lifted his feet from the pavement. It beat his ears with a fistful of snow, and clasped his ribs with icy fingers. It tore the clouds from the sky, and laid bare, as if beyond the darkness, the cold grey envelope of outer space. Heads bent and shoulders thrusting like Rugby forwards in a scrum, east-bound pedestrians struggled against it, and westward travellers flew before it with prodigious strides. To the left, towering blackly, like iron upon the indomitable rock, was the Castle. To it also the storm seemed to have given movement, for as the clouds fled behind its walls the bulk of its ancient towers and battlements appeared to ride slowly in the wind's eye, as

though meditating a journey down the cavernous channel
of the High Street to Holyroodhouse, its deserted sister.[71]

It seems strange, therefore, that the Princes Street Promenade should be an Edinburgh tradition. It was something
that both Thomas Carlyle at the beginning of the nineteenth
century and Edwin Muir in his book *Scottish Journey* (1935) a
century later particularly noticed. Its particular characteristic
Muir noted was 'not only to observe, but also to be observed,
and if you omit one of these duties you strike at its amour-
propre and perhaps at its existence'.[72]

The Gardens occupy the bed of the Nor' Loch, once famed
for its mammoth eels and innumerable waterfowl. Drained,
they were landscaped at the beginning of the nineteenth
century by the Princes Street Proprietors at the cost of some
£7,000. Walter Scott, who was given a key to the gardens and
used to cross them each day on his way from Castle Street to
the Law Courts, recorded in his journal how his journey was
'through a scene of grandeur and beauty perhaps unequalled,
whether the foreground or distant view is considered'.

Little has changed to this day. Dramatically the south side
of Princes Street veers into an abyss and one is in a quiet and
grassy oasis. Here are sheltered walkways, rows of inscribed
benches, statues and neatly laid out flowerbeds. In summer
bands and groups play and ice-cream men peddle their wares.
Something of the atmosphere is captured in Robert Garioch's
poem 'In Princes Street Gardens':

> Down by the baundstaund, by the ice-cream barrie,
> there is a sait that says, Wilma is Fab.
> Sit doun aside me and gieze your gab,
> just you and me, a doun, and a weecock-sparrie.[73]

At the western edge of the Gardens, in a hollow dell,
is St Cuthbert's Church. It is the graveyard, however,
where among others Thomas De Quincey is buried, that
immediately grabs the attention. Steep steps lead past austere
carved figures to walled gardens lined with huge mausoleums.
Above, the Castle throws eerie shadows through the trees on
the ground, while at the foot of the graveyard the trains
hurtle past.

The last memorial in Princes Street is a large granite Celtic cross in memory of Dean Ramsay (1793–1872), the minister of the adjacent St John's Scottish Episcopal Church. His *Reminiscences of Scottish Life and Character* was one of the bestsellers of the day going through twenty editions. Built in 1817 St John's has a splendid interior modelled on St George's Chapel, Windsor. Among those buried there with literary connections are Sir Henry Raeburn, Sir Walter Scott's mother and the novelist Catherine Sinclair.[74]

Charlotte Square with its clasical Corinthian pillars, balustrades, circular panels and windows, is perhaps the crowning achievement of Robert Adam and one of the most beautiful of European squares. It has, however, few literary connections.

Most of the buildings are now occupied by offices, while No 6 is the official residence of the Secretary of State for Scotland. Next door, No 7 has been restored to its original splendour and is now a museum, known as the Georgian House, in the care of the National Trust for Scotland, with the official residence of the Moderator of the General Assembly of the Church of Scotland on the upper floors. Distinguished former residents include the pioneer of antiseptic surgery, Joseph Lister, at No 9; Sir William Fettes, the founder of the school that bears his name at No 13; and Lord Cockburn at No 14.

Henry Cockburn (1779–1854) provides in *Memorials of His Time* a fascinating picture of Edinburgh at the beginning of the nineteenth century. In his duality of outlook he perhaps also stands as a representative Edinburgh figure. He looked back with fond regret at the expansion of the city and yet realised the need for social change. He was part of the Establishment, yet had a hankering for the low life. He felt Scottish but yet had closer affinities with the English.

Walter Scott, Cockburn's almost direct contemporary and neighbour, was able to articulate many of these conflicts in his numerous novels. Scott took lodgings on the second floor of No 108 George Street, for a few weeks after his marriage in 1797, before moving with his wife Charlotte to 10 South Castle Street and eventually to 39 North Castle Street, which was to remain his town house for the next twenty-eight years.

The house, now offices, is clearly identifiable with an inscription at the front, above the bow window, and a bust of Scott visible through a fanlight above the door. It was from this house that Scott left each morning to discharge his official duties at Parliament House and from here many of his books were written. There are numerous descriptions of the house and in particular his study which had

> a single Venetian window opening on a patch of turf not much larger than itself and the aspect of the place was sombrous. The walls were entirely clothed with books, most of them folios and quartos . . . A dozen volumes or so, needful for immediate purposes of reference, were placed close by him on a small moveable frame . . . All the rest were in their proper niches, and wherever a volume had been lent, its room was occupied by a wooden block of the same size, having a card with the name of the borrower and date of the loan, tacked on its front. . . The only table was a massive piece of furniture which he had constructed on the model of one at Rokeby, with a desk and all its appurtenances on either side that an amanuensis might work opposite to him when he chose . . . His own writing apparatus was a very handsome old box richly carved, and lined with crimson velvet, and containing ink-bottles, taper—stand, etc in silver . . . The room had no place for pictures, except one, an original portrait of Claverhouse, which hung over the chimney-piece with a Highland target on either side, and broadswords and dirks (each having its own story) dispersed star fashion round them.[75]

It was here Scott lived while at the peak of his success. When he had to leave it after his financial problems in 1826 he was heart-broken as he noted in his journal:

> March 15—This morning I leave No 39 Castle Street, for the last time . . . In all my former changes of residence it was from good to better; this is retrograding. I leave this house for sale, and I cease to be an Edinburgh citizen, in the sense of being a proprietor, which my father and I have been for sixty years at least. So farewell, poor 39.[76]

Some thirty years later another writer was to live almost

SIR WALTER SCOTT'S HOUSE
CASTLE STREET

opposite. The author of *The Wind in the Willows* (1908), Kenneth Grahame (1859–1932) was born at 32 North Castle Street. His father was a lawyer and used to make the same journey as Scott to the Law Courts each day. In 1860 Grahame senior was made a Sheriff in Argyll and the family left Edinburgh never to return.[77]

The poet Albert Mackie (1904–1985) was living at 34 North Castle Street when he published his first book *Poems in Two Tongues*. Mackie, editor of the *Edinburgh Evening Dispatch* immediately after the Second World War, was in fact a Leith man; born in Brunswick Road he had been brought up in Gayfield Square and Street.

George Street has a distinguished population of statues—the theologian Dr Chalmers, King George IV, William Pitt—which strangely all face south, for the best views are to be had to the north, down the steep slopes towards the Firth of Forth.

It was these views down to the Forth and across to Fife which Alexander Smith especially noted.

> From George Street, which crowns the ridge, the eye is led down sweeping streets of stately architecture to the villas and woods that fill the lower ground, and fringe the shore; to the bright azure belt of the Forth with its smoking steamer or its creeping sail, and beyond, to the shores of Fife, soft blue, and flecked with fleeting shadows in the keen clear light of spring, dark purple in the summer heat, tarnished gold in the autumn haze; and farther away still, just distinguishable on the paler sky, the crest of some distant peak, carrying the imagination into the illimitable world.[78]

Half-way along George Street are the Assembly Rooms built in 1787 and extended at various times in the next century. A focus at one time of the social life of the New Town with its regular dancing assemblies, it has entered literary history for it was here at a dinner of the Edinburgh Theatrical Association in February 1827 that Scott first publicly admitted he was the author of the 'Waverley' novels.

Scott had started work on his novel about the 1745 Jacobite Rising in 1805. Both his publisher James Ballantyne and a close friend Lord Kinedder had disliked the book and Scott abandoned it for several years. After moving to Abbotsford, Scott revised it and in 1814 Constable published *Waverley* with considerable success. By the end of the year it had sold 5,000 copies and made Scott £2,000. Its author however remained the 'Great Unknown'.

A number of explanations have been forwarded for why Scott should wish to remain anonymous. As a Clerk to the Court of Session, Scott may have felt it rather unbecoming to be also a novelist. Equally he may have simply preferred to keep his public life and private interests quite separate.

By 1827 'the author of *Waverley*' had published twenty-three novels including *Rob Roy* (1817), *Heart of Midlothian* (1818), *Ivanhoe* (1819) and *Quentin Durward* (1823) and his identity was an open secret. The books had been a considerable financial and critical success and Scott now felt no embarrassment in confessing to them.

Charles Dickens (1812–70) gave several readings at the Assembly Rooms in the 1840s and 1850s and after reading his 'A Tale of a Christmas Carol' to a packed audience in the Music Hall in 1858 he remarked:

> I never have forgotten, and I can never forget, that I have the honour to be a burgess and guild-brother of the Corporation of Edinburgh. As long as sixteen or seventeen years ago, the first great public recognition and encouragement I ever received was bestowed on me in this generous and magnificent city—in this city so distinguished in literature and so distinguished in the arts. You will readily believe that I have carried into the various countries I have since traversed and through all my subsequent career, the proud and affectionate remembrance of that eventful epoch in my life; and that coming back to Edinburgh is to me like coming home.[79]

Such affection for Edinburgh from a Londoner may owe much to the fact that his wife's family came from the city. Dickens' father-in-law, George Hogarth, had been a friend of Scott and had married one of the daughters of George Thomson, the poet and friend of Burns; Hogarth's brother-in-law was Scott's printer James Ballantyne.

Dickens had first come to Edinburgh in 1834, sent by the

Morning Chronicle to report on the granting of the freedom of the city to Earl Grey, the force behind the Great Reform Bill. His genius was early recognised by both Cockburn and Jeffrey, the latter of whom arranged for the granting of the City's Freedom and a public dinner in Dickens' honour in 1841.

Percy Bysshe Shelley (1792–1822) lodged for five weeks in 1811 at 60 George Street in a ground- and first-floor flat after running away with his sixteen-year-old sweetheart Harriet Westbrook. They were married at the home of the Revd Joseph Robertson at 225 Canongate that August. The house in George Street remains little changed except for the conversion of the ground floor into a shop and the adding of another storey.

Shelley returned two years later and lodged briefly at 36 Frederick Street with his wife and small child in an attempt to avoid his creditors in the south.

The offices of *Blackwood's Magazine* were from 1830 until 1972 opposite the Assembly Rooms, at 45 George Street; it then moved to Thistle Street and finally ceased publication in 1980. Its contributors during this period included John Galt, Bulwer Lytton, Anthony Trollope, R. D. Blackmore, Henry James, Oscar Wilde, John Buchan (with *The Thirty-Nine Steps*), Walter de la Mare, J. B. Priestley, Ian Hay, Nevil Shute and Neil Munro.

Blackwood published all but one of George Eliot's novels. Her lover G. H. Lewes submitted *Scenes from a Clerical Life* in 1856 and it was immediately accepted. *Adam Bede*, *The Mill on the Floss* and *Silas Marner* quickly followed. In 1862 she moved to the *Cornhill Magazine* with *Romola* for an advance of £10,000 but returned to Blackwood four years later with *Felix Holt*.

Some authors, despite many attempts, never became Blackwood authors. In 1835 and 1836 a fifteen-year-old boy wrote a number of times asking his work to be considered. He even pressed for an interview declaring 'a journey of three hundred miles shall not deter me'. His entreaties went unanswered perhaps, as one subsequent commentator noted, because of 'the faint but authentic undertones of madness' in the letters. The young boy was Patrick Brontë.

Later Blackwood turned down a book by H.G. Wells, sending to Wells' agent, a letter that has a modern ring to it:

> Though very well written, I am sorry to say I am not impressed by it. The price he demands for the serial issue seems to me quite prohibitive: likewise the advance on account of royalties on publication. The sum mentioned seems to me excessive for the work after it has appeared in serial form.[80]

Conan Doyle offered the magazine several stories and in 1888, after *Micah Clarke* had been turned down, wrote:

> Your note about *Micah Clarke* is so very kind that I cannot help thinking that you must have debated in your own mind whether you should or should not bring it out. If by meeting you in any way I could alter your decision I should be quite ready to trust to the success of the work for my own revenue, allowing the expences [*sic*] of publication to be defrayed out of the sale first, and then the profits to be divided in such a way as to its success myself. As an Edinburgh man I should be very glad if my first solid book should appear through you.[81]

In the event Blackwood failed to recognise Conan Doyle's promise and published only one of his stories, 'A Physiologist's Wife'; even then they kept it fifteen months.

Another difficult relationship was with Joseph Conrad, who wrote to William Blackwood on 8 February 1899 from Hythe:

> When I sit down to write for you I feel as if in a friendly atmosphere, untrammelled like one is with people that understand, of whom one is perfectly sure. It is a special mood, and a most enjoyable one. Well, I must get on with the wretched novel which seems to have no end and whose beginning I declare I've forgotten. It is a weird sensation; the African nightmare feeling I've tried to put into *Heart of Darkness* is a mere trifle to it.[82]

In October that year *Blackwood*'s published the opening chapters of *Lord Jim*. The magazine exercised great patience with the novelist lending him money and paying for stories that were sometimes never delivered. By 1903 that patience was exhausted and the association ended. In many ways it marked the end of an era and *Blackwood's Magazine* was never as influential in the twentieth century as it had been in the previous one.

On the corner of Hanover Street and Rose Street stands Milne's Bar, one of the most famous literary bars in Edinburgh. There is little now to belie its heritage. It is, however, the framed photographs on the other walls that catch one's attention. Sydney Goodsir Smith, Robert Garioch, Norman MacCaig with, below, respectively their poems 'Never Nae Mair', 'An Alabaster Box', 'November Night'. Nearby is Sorley MacLean and 'Springtide' and Hugh MacDiarmid and 'In an Edinburgh Pub'.

Milne's Bar, throughout the 1950s and 1960s was the meeting place of a whole generation of poets and acolytes dedicated to writing in the Scots tongue and therefore can be said to be almost the centre of the Scots Literary Renaissance. Alasdair Gray in his novel 1982, *Janine* has a scene in the bar, the unholy trinity of which were MacDiarmid, MacCaig and Smith:

> The bar was crowded except where three men stood in a small open space created by the attention of the other customers. One had a sombre pouchy face and upstanding hair which seemed too like thistledown to be natural, one looked like a tall sarcastic lizard, one like a small sly shy bear. 'Our three best since Burns', a bystander informed me, 'barring Sorley, of course.'[83]

Sorley MacLean (1911–), who writes as Somhairle MacGillEain, is now regarded as one of Scotland's greatest Gaelic poets. Born on the island of Raasay he came to Edinburgh in 1929 to study English at the University. It was while training to be a schoolmaster that he met Christopher Murray Grieve (Hugh MacDiarmid) (1892–1978), in Rutherford's. The two immediately struck up a friendship that lasted until MacDiarmid's death.

MacLean first appeared with Garioch in *Seventeen Poems for Sixpence* (1940) and his first solo work was published in

THE Abbotsford BAR
ROSE STREET

Richard Demarco

A RUSH OF POETS AT MILNES BAR
ON THE CORNER OF ROSE AND HANOVER STREETS   Richard Demarco 92

November 1943 under the title *Dain do Eimhir agus Dain Eile*.
It was not, however, until his inclusion in *Four Points of a
Saltire* in 1970 that he became known to a general audience.

MacLean taught at Boroughmuir High School between
1939 and 1940 and then from 1943 to 1956 before becoming
headmaster of Plockton Secondary School in Skye until his
retirement in 1972.[84]

Norman MacCaig (1910–   ), as his *Collected Poems* shows,
has written widely about the city of his birth and is a
sharp observer of its foibles. Born in London Street his
family moved shortly afterwards to Dundas Street where
his father ran a chemist's shop. He was educated at the Royal
High School and then read classics at Edinburgh University
between 1928 and 1932. A Headmaster of Juniper Green
Primary School, and now retired, he has spent his entire life
in the city.

Sydney Goodsir Smith (1915–75) came to Edinburgh at
the age of twelve. Like MacCaig and Robert Garioch he was
educated at the Royal High School and Edinburgh University
and spent his entire life in the city, where for a time he was
the Art Critic of the *Scotsman*. For many years he lived at 50
Craigmillar Park, the 'Schloss Schmidt', and there is a plaque
to him at 25 Drummond Place, his home towards the end of
his life.

Smith's poetry in its vibrant depiction of low life harks back
to the work of Ramsay and Fergusson. MacDiarmid thought
his linguistic romp *Carotid Cornucopious* was 'the best thing
that has ever been written about Edinburgh'.

> . . . the awareness of James Joyce and most other *avant-garde*
> writers, and above all of Jarry's *Ubu Roi* has clearly been
> superadded to the recaptured spirit of Dunbar, Sir Thomas
> Urquhart, and Burns.[85]

Its flavour and authenticity is apparent in the names of some
of the bars that the central character visits—the Abbotsfork
and the Haw-Haw Hures at Quaenisfanny.

The city also figures in three conversational poems *The
Vision of the Prodigal Son* (1960), *Kynd Kittock's Land* (1965)
and *Gowdspink in Reekie* (1974).

Among the distinguished visitors to Milne's Bar were Stevie

Smith, Dylan Thomas and W. H. Auden who arrived in his slippers and his cups. So famous did the gatherings at Milne's Bar become that 'the Rose Street poets' adjourned a few yards east to a much more elegant establishment, the Abbotsford.

With its ornate plaster work, island bar and wooden panelling the Abbotsford remains much as it was when it was patronised in the 1960s. The writer Alan Bold (1943–   ), who knew the circle, has recalled

> MacDiarmid alternating between affability and intensity, MacCaig delivering swift sarcastic verbal thrusts, Smith with a monocle in his eye and a glass in his hand and sometimes an inhaler at his throat to ward off attacks of asthma. All three poets were incessant smokers as well as heavy drinkers so their presence was surrounded by a tobacco cloud of unknowing. [86]

Bold, though he now lives in Fife, is one of the most prolific and interesting contemporary Edinburgh writers. Born and brought up at the top of Leith Walk he was educated at Broughton High School, like his great hero MacDiarmid, and Edinburgh University. For many years he worked as a journalist before taking up writing full-time. In addition to his award-winning biography of MacDiarmid, he has compiled a series of anthologies and written widely on Scottish culture, as well as being a distinguished poet.

St Andrew Square was, until recent dispersal to purpose-built offices, the financial centre of the capital. No 35, now Barclay's Bank, was where the dying Sir Walter Scott spent his last two nights in Edinburgh on his return from Italy in July 1832 when it was Douglas's Hotel. Scott knew the area already. After his bankruptcy and the death of his wife he had spent two months in the lodging house of a Mrs Brown round the corner at 6 North St David Street.

This leads into Queen Street, one of the New Town's finest residential streets. Sydney Smith (1771–1845), one of the founders of the *Edinburgh Review* lived for a time at No 19 before moving after his marriage to 46 George Street. He had come to Edinburgh in 1798 to act as a private tutor and first lodged at 38 Hanover Street.

Smith lived in Edinburgh until 1804 and always had warm feelings about the capital. He wrote:

> With Edinburgh I am delighted as surprised, though it is offensive to the nose as it is delightful to the eye. No smells were ever equal to Scotch smells; it is the school of physic. Yet the place is uncommonly beautiful and I am in a constant balance between admiration and trepidation. . . . Never shall I forget the happy days passed there, amidst odious smells, barbarous sounds, bad suppers, excellent hearts and most enlightened and cultivated understandings.[87]

John Wilson, 'Christopher North', resided with his mother at No 53, even after his marriage, before moving to 29 Ann Street in 1819 and his final home, 6 Gloucester Place, in 1826. Next door at 52 Queen Street chloroform was discovered at the home of Dr James Young Simpson.

It was at the Philosophical Institution in Queen Street that John Ruskin (1819–1900), whose family came from Edinburgh, delivered his famous series of lectures in November 1853.

In 1884 Oscar Wilde (1854–1900) gave two lectures in the Queen Street Hall. *The Picture of Dorian Gray* is supposed to have been based on Father John Gray (1866–1934), a priest at St Peter's Church, Falcon Avenue, whom Wilde had met in London in 1889. Gray's first collection of poems *Silverpoints* (1893) were paid for by Wilde.

Eric Linklater's Magnus Merriman lived in Queen St in:

> a row of tall flatfronted houses whose residential dignity had been somewhat impaired by the invasion of offices and a few shops of a superior kind. His flat was at the top of the house and its windows looked north across gardens and a descending terrace of intersecting streets to a mistiness that in fine weather dissolved and revealed the steely brightness of the Forth. Beyond that were the ancient kingdom of Fife, soberly coloured, and the rising blue shadow of the Ochil hills, that outpost of the Highlands and a promise of farther heights.[88]

Linklater knew this area well for during the early 1930s he

shared a flat at 11 York Place. The portrait painter Henry Raeburn had his studios in York Place, interconnecting Queen Street with Picardy Place, which takes its name from a colony of Picardy silk weavers, established here in the seventeenth century.

Arthur Ignatius Conan Doyle was born in May 1859 at 11 Picardy Place. His father Charles worked for the Scottish Office of Works and had designed the small statues of historical figures for the fountain of Holyroodhouse; his mother Mary was distantly related to Walter Scott. Though Charles supplemented his income by sketching for magazines and books, money was scarce and he failed to exercise his parental responsibilities. An epileptic, he eventually took to drink and was committed to Crichton Royal Institution, a mental hospital near Dumfries, where he died in 1893.

The Conan Doyle birthplace was pulled down in the 1960s to make room for the huge roundabout at the top of Leith Walk. The mysteries of Paolozzi's sculptures outside St Mary's R. C. Cathedral are pondered by a recently erected statue of Sherlock Holmes. A plaque opposite, on the surviving side of the street, marks the house.[89]

To the north of Queen Street lies the first extension of the New Town begun at the turn of the nineteenth century and largely completed by 1823. Dundas Street provided the north/south axis with Heriot Row, Northumberland Street and Abercromby Place the cross-bars. Finally, on land, originally belonging to the Earl of Moray, a series of beautiful crescents and streets were built, that are now among the best addresses in Edinburgh–Randolph Crescent, Ainslie Place and Moray Place.

Next door to the Moray Estate is Heriot Row. Elizabeth Grant of Rothiemurchus noted when she took lodgings there at the beginning of the nineteenth century:

> There were no prettily laid out gardens then between Heriot Row and Queen Street, only a long strip of unsightly grass, a green, fenced by an untidy wall and abandoned to the use of the washer-women. It was an ugly prospect, and we were daily indulged with it, the cleanliness of the

inhabitants being so excessive that, except on Sundays and 'Saturdays at e'en' squares of bleaching linens and lines of drying ditto were ever before our eyes.[90]

By the middle of the century all that had changed and the Gardens are amongst the prettiest sights in Edinburgh. Moray McLaren has written 'Edinburgh is a city of autumn. It is her best and loveliest season. Sunset transfigures her as it does few other places'.[91] The sight of the Castle etched against the fiery evening sky or the Calton Hill glowing above Princes Street once seen is never forgotten.

McLaren's novel *The Pursuit* beautifully captures this particular quality of Edinburgh:

> The town was bathed in that luminous silver and pale gold glow which the northern autumn alone can produce. There are always one or two days of this exquisitely peaceful benevolence even after the great storms break and before the purgatory of an Edinburgh winter begins. The trees in the Heriot Row gardens that had of late been bending beneath the wind stood motionless and delicate as filigree. Their discarded leaves lay heaped in brown, yellow, and here and there crimson on the grass of the gardens and in the streets. The sky was of the palest most flawless blue. Even the grey Georgian houses facing uphill and into the south had lost their severity and had, in the deep, silver interstices of their stones, caught something of the sunlight in which they had been bathed all day long.[92]

Heriot Row is a dignified street, huge houses with neat front doors and the brass plaques that advertise this street of advocates. The lawyers have begun to leave, the houses to be divided but the splendour remains. One of the central characters of the *The Pursuit*, Fleming–Stewart lives in Heriot Row and is well aware of its hidden resonances. He leads a visitor to the window.

> 'Out there in those gardens about ninety years ago a small boy played by himself and made up dreams, some of them pleasantly adventurous, some of them evil. Later on when he was about thirty, he wrote what he called 'A Shilling Shocker' entirely concerned with the problems of evil. It

R. L. STEVENSON'S HOUSE   Richard Demarco '92

has plenty of absurdities and betises in it—and some fine phrases. It's fantastic and incredible, but it took the English-reading world by storm and is still a favourite plot.'

'I know,' said Jim, 'R. L. Stevenson's *Dr Jekyll and Mr Hyde*. He lived here in Heriot Row.'

'Precisely. But he couldn't have written it if he hadn't known Edinburgh in his bones. This aristocratic, respectable old city of ours has a tradition of subterranean evil which it has not yet shaken off.'[93]

That boy was Robert Louis Stevenson who moved from Inverleith Terrace to live at 17 Heriot Row in 1856. Each night his faithful nurse Cummy would carry him to the nursery window and point out the lights in the Queen Street houses where perhaps also 'there might be sick little boys and their nurses, waiting like us for the morning'. He would look out of the window for Leerie the Lamplighter 'for we are very lucky, with a lamp before the door'. A verse from 'Leerie the Lamplighter' is inscribed on the railings by the front door.

The four-storey Georgian terraced house, still in private hands, bears a close resemblance to that 'citadel of the proprieties', the house in Stevenson's highly autobiographical story 'The Misadventures of John Nicholson'.

It was from Heriot Row that Stevenson made his way to school, first to Mr Henderson's School round the corner in India Street, then to Edinburgh Academy in Henderson Row, founded in the early 1820s by Henry Cockburn and another advocate Leonard Horner. Both men had felt that the Greek instruction at the High School, which they had both attended, was not of sufficiently high a standard to compete with the growing number of English public schools. As a result many parents were beginning to send their sons south to school. Both men were Whigs and realised that if their plans were to succeed they must enlist the support of the Tories which is how Sir Walter Scott became involved in the enterprise. Scott, then at the height of his fame, served as a Director until 1832 and made the principle speech at the opening ceremony. Very quickly the school established itself as one of the leading educational establishments in the city.

Stevenson started at the school in the autumn of 1861 aged

THE EDINBURGH ACADEMY FROM
SILVERMILLS LANE.

Richard Demarco '92

eleven. He seems to have kept very much to himself and made little impact. Two years later he left to join his mother whose poor health meant she had to spend the winter in France.

Stevenson's final school was kept by a Robert Thompson on the west side of Frederick Street. There he was able to develop his individuality so that by the time he left in 1867 he was regarded as quite a non-conformist.

A contemporary leaves this picture of the young Stevenson:

> At that time Louis Stevenson was the queerest looking object you could conceive. To begin with he was badly put together, a slithering, loose flail of a fellow, all joints, elbows, and exposed spindle-shanks, his trousers being generally a foot too short in the leg. He was so like a scarecrow that one almost expected him to creak in the wind. And what struck us all was that he seemed to take a pride in aggravating the oddities of nature. When the weather happened to be fine—and I don't remember seeing him when it wasn't—he came in a battered straw hat that his grandfather must have worn and laid aside because it was out-of-date. Under that antiquated headgear his long, lank hair fell straggling to his shoulders, giving him the look of a quack or gipsy. He wore duck trousers and a black shirt, with loose collar and a tie that might be a strip torn from a cast-away carpet. His jacket was of black velvet and it was noticeable that it never seemed good or new. We remarked among ourselves that there must be a family trunk full of old clothes which he was wearing out.[94]

A short walk away is Drummond Place where a plaque at No 25 commemorates Sydney Goodsir Smith who lived there towards the end of his life. A few doors away at No 28 was the home of Charles Kirkpatrick Sharpe (1791–1851), a friend of Sir Walter Scott. An eccentric Edinburgh figure, whose visiting card bore only the musical notation C sharp, his letters give a good picture of the city during the first part of the nineteenth century. The house was filled with such a vast collection of books and memorabilia, including supposedly part of Robert Bruce's shroud and a tea-caddy used by Mrs M'Lehose, that on his death the auction of the contents lasted six days.

Another writer who lived in Drummond Place was Compton Mackenzie (1883–1972), the author of over a hundred books, including *Sinister Street*, *The Four Winds of Love* and *Whisky Galore*. Mackenzie moved to No 31 in the spring of 1953 and lived there until his death, spending each summer in the South of France.

The house stands on the shoulder of a small rise and on one side looks over its own gardens to the Firth of Forth and on the other across public gardens. Mackenzie lived there with his second wife Chrissie, whom he had married only in 1962, despite having been together for thirty-five years. Shortly afterwards she was diagnosed as having cancer and died in October 1963 at the age of only fifty-four.

In March 1965 he married her sister Lily, who, in 1959 at his suggestion, had opened a hairdressing salon in the basement of No 31, occasioning Evelyn Waugh to write to him 'someone told me a barber had opened up shop in your beautiful house. Surely not?'

Here Mackenzie completed his multi-volume autobiography and here he died on St Andrew's Day 1972, seven weeks short of his ninetieth birthday. He was buried on the Island of Barra where he had lived during the Second World War. At his burial the eighty-two-year-old piper collapsed during the last lament and died a few minutes later.

Just below Drummond Place is Fettes Row where the writer Margaret Oliphant (1828–1897), regarded as Edinburgh's first full-time woman of letters, lived for many years. In her time she was a highly successful and prodigious writer of novels, biographies and articles, many of them for Blackwood's, whose history she wrote. A current resident of Fettes Row is the poet and playwright Stewart Conn (1936–).

THE CALTON HILL   Richard Demarco

The Villa Quarters

One of the most enduring images of the city is Calton Hill. Numerous postcards immortalise its cluster of monuments and photographers seek to capture it from every possible angle. From it can be had some of the best views of Edinburgh. It is therefore appropriate in seeking to satirise Edinburgh's pretensions that Norman MacCaig should take in his poem 'Inward Bound' one of its most prominent symbols:

> On the Calton Hill
> the twelve pillars
> of this failed Parthenon
> made more Greek by the Cargo boat
> sailing between them
> on the cobwebby waters of the Firth
> should marry nicely with the Observatory
> in the way complements do
> each observing the heavens
> in its different way.

MacCaig is referring to the National Monument, modelled on the Parthenon, and designed to commemorate the Scottish soldiers and sailors who had fought in the Napoleonic Wars, its foundation stone was laid by George IV during his visit in 1822, but owing to lack of funds the work was never completed. Subsequently there were plans to finish the monument and dedicate it to Burns, Queen Victoria or turn it into a National Gallery.

Other buildings on Calton Hill include the old City Observatory and the Nelson Monument, built in 1807-8 to mark the victory at Trafalgar. Below on Regent Road is the old Royal High School—described by Sir John Summerson as 'the noblest monument of the Scottish Greek Revival'—which moved here from High School Yards in 1829 and was adapted in the late 1970s to take the proposed Scottish Assembly, a stone's throw from St Andrew's House, the headquarters of the Scottish Office.

On the south side of Regent Road is the Burns Monument. This was where Alexander Smith thought the best views in Edinburgh were to be had, especially at night:

> It is more astonishing than an Eastern dream. A city rises up before you painted by fire on night. High in air a bridge of lights leap the chasm; a few emerald lamps, like glow-worms, are moving silently about in the railway station below; a solitary crimson one is at rest. That ridged and chimneyed bulk of blackness, with splendour bursting out at every pore, is the wonderful Old Town, where Scottish history mainly transacted itself; while, opposite, the modern Princes Street is blazing throughout its length.[95]

Stevenson's parents and grandparents are buried in the New Calton Burying Ground, situated through some black iron gates, beside the monument. The burial ground, which grips the side of the hill, has commanding views across to Salisbury Crags. The Stevenson family grave is a flat-roofed calaboose by the eastern wall, the gates rusty, the walls covered in graffiti. A marble slab in the middle of the floor commemorates Thomas Stevenson and his son:

> Robert Louis Stevenson
> Essayist, Poet, and Novelist
> Born at Edinburgh 13th November 1850
> Died in Samoa 3rd December 1894
> and buried on VAEA Mountain

The Old Calton Burying Ground is little more than a patch of grass at the foot of Calton Hill, just off Waterloo Place. Among those buried there are David Hume and the rival publishers William Blackwood and Archibald Constable.

This part of Edinburgh has many associations with Stevenson. He writes about it most evocatively in *Picturesque Notes* and set a number of scenes from his first novel *The Misadventures of John Nicholson* around the Calton Hill. His uncle Alan, builder of the Skerrymore lighthouse, lived at no 25 Regent Terrace while Greenside Parish Church at the foot of Royal Terrace was for a time the Stevenson family church. Stevenson often worshipped here and has described the church in *Random Memories*.

Stevenson's paternal grandfather lived in a large rambling house with a paddock, 1 Baxter Place, at the top of Leith Walk. The paddock is now a car park and the house, now called Robert Stevenson House, is occupied by a group of publishers. A brass plaque in the hall reads:

> In this building Robert Stevenson, Engineer, lived and worked. From No 1 he designed and supervised many works including bridges, harbours, prisons and light-houses, the most famous of these being the Bell Light-houses. He was the grandfather of Robert Louis Stevenson, Author.

At the corner of the nearby Antigua Street is the stationer's shop, celebrated in *A Penny Plain and Twopence Coloured*.[96]

Broughton Street leads down to Canonmills where, in *Kidnapped*, David Balfour met Alan Breck before they made their dash for the sea.

Stevenson knew the area well having been born at 8 Howard Place, a rather sombre Georgian terrace to the north of Canonmills on the Water of Leith. The two-storey house was small and suffered from damp; it was also far from healthy, given the amount of effluent from the mills and tanneries as well as sewage that was poured into the river. The house in Howard Place was between 1926 and 1963 a museum and the headquarters of the Robert Louis Stevenson Club.

The poet W. E. Henley (1849–1903), a friend and collaborator of Stevenson, lived at 11 Howard Place while editor of the *Scots Observer*. Stevenson based some of Long John Silver on his rumbustious friend and they wrote four plays together in the 1880s, though without much success. Sir J. M. Barrie was a friend and took a particular interest in the Henleys' child Margaret who used to call him 'Friendy-Wendy', the name he was later to immortalise in *Peter Pan*.

Later, another important Edinburgh writer, Lewis Spence (1874–1955), was living at 34 Howard Place. Though born in Dundee Spence came to Edinburgh as a young man to study dentistry at the University. He spent most of his life in the city, where he worked for a time on the *Scotsman*, and where he was a familiar figure in his bowler hat and spats.

Spence was a founding figure with Hugh MacDiarmid of the Scottish Literary Renaissance which aimed to 'bring Scottish literature into closer touch with current European tendencies in technique and ideation' and also of the Scottish National Party.

Round the corner is Warriston Crescent, an attractive cul-de-sac whose houses have gardens running down to the Water of Leith. Frederick Chopin stayed at No 10 when he gave a recital in Queen Street in 1848. Further along at No 25 lives the poet George Bruce (1909-   ), the author of a book on the Edinburgh International Festival, and a BBC producer for over twenty years. His poem 'Houses' ends with a stanza about his own home

> Our house is different; it is very old,
> it creaks a bit in the wind,
> is water-tight now and then,
> comfortable for mice with good runways:
> it should do my time.

Moray McLaren (1901–71), the BBC's first Programme Director for Scotland, lived for many years nearby in Inverleith Row. Educated at Merchiston and Cambridge, McLaren served in the Foreign Office during the Second World War before returning to Edinburgh in 1945. The author of several novels, volumes of short stories and biographies of Boswell and Stevenson he never fully achieved his initial promise. His study of Edinburgh in the twentieth century, *The Capital of Scotland*, is one of the most perceptive accounts of the city.

The Botanical Gardens in Inverleith Place were formed in 1824 when the old 'Physic Gardens' at the foot of the Calton Hill were abolished and now cover over seventy acres. Noman MacCaig has written several poems set in the Botanic Gardens including 'Botanic Gardens' and 'Reclining figure by Henry Moore'.

From the gardens, particularly just in front of Inverleith

House, there are wonderful views to the Castle and Salisbury Crags.

> South of the Rhododendron Walk, from a small eminence
> in the Garden, there is a good broad view of the city,
> reaching from the unfinished Acropolis on the Calton
> Hill to the distant slopes of the Pentlands. The Castle
> on its Rock rises in the midst of the view, and far to
> the left of it Edinburgh's private and domestic mountain,
> Arthur's Seat, is elevated above the Salisbury Crags that
> loom, from here, as if they impended upon the rough
> North Sea. Spires and pinnacles advertise the innumerable
> churches of the city: the two St Georges, the solid burden
> of Playfair's St Stephen's in front of the towering steeple of
> the High Church, St Andrew's and the Tron and the crown
> of St Giles. There is woodland in the foreground, such
> charming woodland, with pine-needles on its little paths
> and blue Tibetan poppies, or yellow primulas, to enliven
> the shadow of the conifers; and always a new prospect of
> trees and flowers as the visitor more deeply invades the
> climbing pattern of the wood.[97]

At the west end of Inverleith Place stands the imposing, if slightly ridiculous, Fettes College. Built by David Bryce in 1870 in what has been called Franco-Scottish Gothic style to provide an English public school education north of the border, the school has produced a number of writers, including W. C. Sellar (1899–1951) the part-author of the comic masterpiece *1066 and All That* and a theatre collaborator with P. G. Wodehouse and Robert Bruce Lockhart (1887–1970) best known for *Memoirs of a British Agent* based on his experiences in Russia during the First World War. According to popular tradition Ian Fleming's character James Bond was sent to Fettes after an indiscretion with a ladies maid at Eton.

Norman Cameron (1905–53) went from Fettes to Oxford in the early 1920s where he became a friend of Robert Graves. After a posting to Nigeria as an educational officer he went to live with Graves and Laura Riding. Cameron was known as a translator of Rimbaud and Villon as well as a poet in his own right. He wrote the introduction to Graves' *Collected Poems*.

The writer Ruthven Todd (1914–) spent several unhappy

years there from 1928, where his contemporaries included the
poet George Campbell Hay. Todd went on to the Edinburgh
College of Art and then worked briefly as a journalist in the
city. Most of his life has been spent in the United States but
he does leave a bitter picture in the autobiographical poem 'In
Edinburgh' (1940).

> I was born in this city of grey stone and bitter wind,
> Of tenements sooted up with lying history:
> This place where dry mounds grow crusts of hate, as
>   rocks
> Grow lichens. I went to school over the high bridge
> Fringed with spikes which curiously, repel the suicides;
> And I slept opposite the rock garden where the
>   survivors,
> Who had left Irving and Mallory under the sheet of
>   snow,
> Planted the incaruillia and saxifrages of the Himalayas.

After the Second World War, during which he was first
a conscientious objector and then invalided out, George
Campbell Hay (1916–84) worked in the Department of
Printed Books in the National Library of Scotland. Between
1947 and his death Hay published four collections of poetry,
much of it in Gaelic.

Two streets to the south is Comely Bank where Thomas
Carlyle began his married life at No 21 in 1826. This leads
into Raeburn Place and then Deanhaugh Street where James
Hogg lodged in 1813. If one climbs Dean Terrace, the Water
of Leith running alongside to the left, one comes first of
all to Danube Street. Until it was closed in the mid-1970s,
17 Danube Street was the site of Edinburgh's best-known
brothel. Its madame, Dora Noyce, who ran it from 1943 until
her death in 1977, bears more than a passing resemblance to
Ma Blinkbonnie and her salon in Bruce Marshall's novel *The
Black Oxen*. Hector Macmillan's 'play with music', *Capital
Offence*, staged at the Royal Lyceum in 1981, is also based on
the brothel.

As with so much in Edinburgh the dubious and the
respectable are in close proximity. Above Danube Street is

Ann Street. Built between 1816 and 1823 the street was named
after the wife of the portrait painter Sir Henry Raeburn, who
owned the land. The street stands in contrast to the stern and
somewhat forbidding beauty of the surrounding eighteenth-
century streets. The two rows of what look like dolls' houses,
with their brightly coloured doors and landscaped gardens,
combine to make this one of the prettiest and most exclusive
residential streets in Edinburgh.

John Wilson moved to 29 Ann Street in 1819 and there De
Quincey lodged for a year after coming in one night to
shelter from the rain. It was at 25 Ann Street, two doors
down, that the future author of *Coral Island* R. M. Ballantyne
(1825–1894) was born. His family had moved to Edinburgh
the year before on the appointment of his father as editor of
the *Edinburgh Weekly Journal*, first staying for a few months at
25 Comely Bank.

Ballantyne's uncle, James, was Sir Walter Scott's publisher
and after the 1826 crash when both Scott and James Ballantyne
were ruined the whole Ballantyne family were forced to move
to Regent Moray's House in the Canongate; this they shared
with David Cowan, a partner in the paper-making firm they
used. It was only when Scott had paid back his debts that the
Ballantyne family were able to move again, this time settling
at 20 Fettes Row.

The other side of the street also has several literary associations. The two daughters of the critic David Masson, Flora
and Rosaline, both authors in their own right lived at No 11,
while Robert Chambers, the author of *Traditions of Edinburgh*
lived at No 28 between 1834 and 1838.

Helen Bannerman (1862–1946), the author of *Little Black
Sambo* (1899), left her four children with her sister Mary at
50 Ann Street to complete their education while she stayed
in India with her doctor husband. Born at 35 Royal Terrace
and educated in Edinburgh, Bannerman left for India on her
marriage in 1889, retiring to Edinburgh in 1918, where she
remained until her death.[99]

Dean Park Crescent leads on to the Dean Bridge which towers
some 100 ft above the Water of Leith.[100] Bell's Brae, once the

main road to the north, descends steeply into the gorge to the picturesque Dean Village below. Here Stevenson's Catriona lived with Lady Allardyce 'in a decentlike small house in a garden of lawns and appletrees'. The weavers' cottages on Damside were pulled down by the proprietor of the *Scotsman*, John Ritchie Findlay, because they spoilt the view from his house in Rothesay Terrace. They have now been replaced by Well Court which, with its gables and large tower, makes a pleasant contrast with the surrounding village.

From the village one can walk along the Water of Leith, west in the direction of the Scottish National Gallery of Modern Art, or east towards Stockbridge. A few hundred yards towards the latter is St Bernard's Well which was refurbished at the beginning of the nineteenth century by the publisher, William Nelson, who used to walk three miles a day to drink the dark sulphurous waters.

The writer J. K. Annand (1908-) was born next door to St Bernard's Well at 11 Mackenzie Place, now known as St Bernard's Cottages, and lived there until his marriage in 1936. Annand's reputation rests largely on his Scots verse for children *Sing it Aince for Pleasure* (1965), *Thrice for Joy* (1974) and *Twice to Show Ye* (1979).

From the Dean Village, Dean Path climbs the other side of the valley until it returns to Queensferry Road at the Dean Cemetery. Among those buried there are Henry Cockburn, Francis Jeffrey, John Wilson and his son-in-law William Aytoun. Dean House, which was demolished to make way for the construction of the cemetery in 1845, was the scene of the novel *Miller of Denhaugh* by James Ballantine (1808–1877).

To the south of Queensferry Road, in Ravelston Dykes Road, is New Ravelston House, which was built in 1791. Now part of the Mary Erskine School for Girls, its terraces, grass walks and statues once provided the inspiration for Tullyveolan in Scott's *Waverley*.

Opposite the school is the start of a public footpath which climbs the wooded slopes of Corstorphine Hill between Murrayfield and Ravelston golf courses. On the Ravelston side of the hill is the viewpoint of 'Rest and Be Thankful' where David Balfour parted from Alan Breck in Stevenson's

ST. BERNARD'S WELL,   Richard Demarco '92

Kidnapped. On the 529 ft summit is Clermiston Tower, now boarded up, which was built in 1871 to mark the centenary of Sir Walter Scott's birth.

On the other side of the hill, in Craigcrook Road, is Craigcrook Castle which has a number of literary associations. Archibald Constable lived there at the beginning of the nineteenth century selling it to Lord Jeffrey in 1815.[101] Cockburn thought 'No unofficial house in Scotland has had a greater influence on literary or political opinion'.[102] Certainly most of the leading literary figures of the day have visited it including Tennyson, Dickens, Hans Christian Anderson, George Eliot and Thackeray.

Craigcrook Road leads into Queensferry Road which in turn becomes Queensferry Street and Shandwick Place. Scott lived at 6 Shandwick Place from November 1827 until his retirement from the Clerkship of Session in July 1830 when he moved to Abbotsford permanently. Scott also lived for a period at 3 Walker Street and 16 Atholl Crescent, the home of his publisher Robert Cadell. Cadell had formerly been a partner in his father-in-law's firm Constable but after the failure of Constable and the partnerships were dissolved Cadell purchased the copyright of the Scott novels from *Waverley* to *Quentin Durward* for £8,500 and then published an 'Author's edition' which was highly successful. Scott wrote in his journal at the time of the break:

> Constable without Cadell is like getting the clock without the pendulum; the one having the ingenuity, the other the caution of the business.[103]

Across the road in Palmerston Place is St Mary's Episcopal Cathedral and the novelist Fred Urquhart (1912-), the son of a chauffeur who features as the character Jim Lovat in the autobiographical *Palace of Green Days* (1979) was born at No 8.

In 1919 the family moved to 37 West Cottages, Granton, which figures in his novel *Time Will Knit* (1938). The cottages, which were between the middle and west piers, were demolished before the Second World War. Urquhart later lived at 1 and then 10 Fraser Grove, off Granton Road.

Leaving Broughton High School at fifteen Urquhart worked for seven years in Cairns' Bookshop in Teviot Place and for a firm of tailors in George Street, an experience which he used in his story 'Sweet', collected in *I Fell for a Sailor* (1940). Subsequently Urquhart had a series of jobs in publishing working as a literary agent in London, a reader for MGM, a scout for Walt Disney and an editor for Cassell. His novel *Jezebel's Dust* (1951) is set in Edinburgh.

The area to the north and west of Lothian Road is a mixture of neighbourhoods. Along Lothian Road itself are situated various cinemas and Edinburgh's principal theatre, the Royal Lyceum and concert hall, the Usher Hall. Named after the head of a brewing family who gave £100,000 in 1896 to 'promote and extend the cultivation of, and taste for, music, not only in Edinburgh, but throughout the country' the Usher Hall was completed in 1911.

In his poem 'Choral Symphony' Stewart Conn casts a witty look at the sort of audience the Usher Hall might attract:

> The customary conversation
> Gives way to applause
> For the Orchestra. Then
> A roar, as Karajan
> Takes the stand. He raises
> His baton; the strings sweep in.
>
> During the interval, we remain
> Seated. Two Edinburgh ladies
> Behind us complain:
> 'Such Teutonic discipline
> Breeds perfection,
> Not Art.' Their companion agrees.
>
> At the end they join in,
> As the ovation goes on
> And on. What has changed their tune?
> We overhear:'Weren't the Chorus
> Superb!' 'As one voice.'
> 'And that lace, on Muriel's dress.'

Since its inauguration in 1947 the Edinburgh International

Festival has done much to promote Scottish writing and writers, as well as introduce music, drama and art from around the world. Robert Kemp's adaptations of the sixteenth-century classic *The Thrie Estaitis* and Allan Ramsay's *The Gentle Shepherd* and his own play *The Other Dear Charmer* were great successes. There have been adaptations of Hogg's *The Confessions of a Justified Sinner* and revivals of Home's *Douglas* as well as new plays by James Bridie, Eric Linklater and Sydney Goodsir Smith and tributes to Walter Scott and Hugh MacDiarmid. Stephen Macdonald's play about Wilfred Owen and Siegfried Sassoon, *Not About Heroes* was a hit of the 1982 Festival Fringe, while more recently there has been a dramatisation of the relationship between W. E. Henley and R. L. Stevenson.[104]

The dual sides to the Edinburgh character are never better expressed than in Muriel Spark's novel *The Prime of Miss Jean Brodie*. One theme in the book is the huge disparity in wealth in the city, and how the more fortunate view the unemployed. In the following passage the girls are out walking in the area called Tollcross:

> They had come to the end of Lauriston Place, past the fire station, where they were to get on a tram-car to go to tea with Miss Brodie in her flat at Church Hill. A very long queue of men lined this part of the street. They were without collars, in shabby suits. They were talking and spiting and smoking little bits of cigarette held between middle finger and thumb.
>
> 'We shall cross here,' said Miss Brodie and herded the set across the road.
>
> Monica Douglas whispered, 'They are the Idle.'
>
> 'In England they are called the Unemployed. They are waiting to get their dole from the labour bureau,' said Miss Brodie. 'You must all pray for the unemployed and their families, I will write you out the special prayer for them . . . Sometimes they go and spend their dole on drink before they go home, and their children starve. They are our brothers, Sandy, stop staring at once. In Italy the unemployment problem has been solved.'[105]

This is still one of the poorer parts of Edinburgh but large parts of the area have benefited from redevelopment in recent years.

In Bruce Marshall's panoramic novel about three generations of an Edinburgh family in the twentieth century, *The Black Oxen* (1972), this tale of two cities is again made clear. The five male characters go to a 'brightly lit dancing hall in Fountainbridge', most probably the old Palais:

> Inside, the orchestra was playing 'Oh, Oh, My Sweet Hortense' and on the dance floor a mixed bag of semi-sober advocates, Writers to the Signet, solicitors to the Supreme Court, chartered accountants, students and keellies were revolving with a kaleidoscope of typists, instructresses, brickfaced Murrayfield heiresses and lugubrious tarts.[106]

There, one of them, Neil Duncan meets and falls in love with Flora Goodwillie but the path of love does not run smoothly for, as he is told, 'future members of the Edinburgh Stock Exchange don't marry dancing instructresses'. Flora has to point out what is more than a geographical separation: 'You live in Murrayfield and I live at the foot of Leith Walk.'

Though Bruce Marshall (1899–   ) spent much of his life in France, many of his books have an Edinburgh setting. They include *Teacup Terrace* (1926), *Father Malachy's Miracle* (1931) and *George Brown's Schooldays* (1946). After the First World War, during which he lost a leg, and Edinburgh University he worked as an accountant for fourteen years in Paris. During the Second World War he joined SOE where he met the Resistance hero Yeo–Thomas, the subject of Marshall's bestseller *The White Rabbit*.

Bruntsfield Links, has long associations with the game of golf and there have been clubs there for two centuries, though the famous Bruntsfield Links Golfing Society now has a course near Barnton. Smollett writes of Edinburgh golfers in *The Expedition of Humphry Clinker*:

> Among others, I was shown one particular set of golfers, the youngest of whom was turned four score. They were all gentlemen of independent fortunes, who had amused themselves with this pastime for the best part of a century,

THE GOLF TAVERN
BRUNTSFIELD

Richard Demarco '92

without having ever felt the least alarm from sickness or disgust, and they never went to bed without having each the best part of a gallon of claret. Such uninterrupted exercise, co-operating with the keen air from the sea, must, without all doubt, keep the appetite always on edge, and steel the constitution against all the common attacks of distemper.[107]

The claret was no doubt sampled at the Golf Tavern which for five centuries now has provided the nineteenth hole for those who, in Allan Ramsay's words, 'were weary'd at the gowff'.

Muriel Spark (1918–), born Muriel Camberg, was brought up in Bruntsfield Place and attended James Gillespie's School for Girls, which she supposedly took as her model for the Marcia Blaine School in *The Prime of Miss Jean Brodie*. Though most of her life has been spent outside the city Spark has conceded that 'Edinburgh had an effect on my mind, my prose style and my ways of thought.'

Another contemporary female 'Edinburgh' writer is Joan Lingard whose novel *The Prevailing Wing*, is based on her experiences as a student living in Warrender Park Terrace in the 1950s. *The Headmaster* (1967) is set in the neighbouring Grange. Lingard, who lived for a time in Chalmers Crescent, uses Edinburgh in several other novels most notably *A Sort of Freedom* (1969), *The Gooseberry* (1978) and *The Second Flowering of Emily Mountjoy* (1979).

Few now realise that the girls' school immortalised in the cartoons of Ronald Searle and the films starring Alastair Sim really did exist. Founded at 10 Palmerston Road, off Chalmers Crescent, in 1922 St Trinnean's soon earned a reputation as 'the school where they do what they like'. While liberal in its approach it was essentially serious-minded and there is no record of teachers being strung up or girls running riot.

Though Searle never met its redoubtable first headmistress Miss C. Fraser Lee, he first learnt of the school while billeted in 1941 with a family in Kirkcudbright, whose two daughters attended St Trinnean's. In July his first cartoon based on the school was published in *Lilliput* but it was not until Searle's return from a Japanese POW camp in 1946 that the school

JAMES GILLESPIE'S HIGH SCHOOL
AND THE MEADOWS

Richard Demarco '72

properly entered public consciousness. The school moved to St Leonard's House in Dalkeith Road in 1925 and to Galashiels in 1939. It became a casualty of the war and closed in 1946.[108]

Another school nearby is George Watson's which moved to Colinton Road in 1932, after over a hundred years in Lauriston Place. It has produced rather more cabinet ministers than writers but its alumni include the critics William Archer and David Daiches. Jessie Saxby's novel *Ben Hanson* (1884) is set at the school.[109]

Further down Colinton Road is Craiglockhart, now an extension of Napier Polytechnic of Edinburgh. Built in 1865 as a poorhouse by the City of Edinburgh Parochial Board it became in 1880 the Craiglockhart Hydropathic Institution and then in the summer of 1916 a Military Hospital under the auspices of the Red Cross.

Wilfred Owen arrived the following summer and quickly threw himself into the activities on offer including editing the *Hydra*, the Hospital magazine. The eighth issue lists the arrival of 2nd Lt Siegfried Sassoon of the Royal Welch Fusiliers. The extraordinary coincidence of two of the First World War's most important poets being sent to the same hospital to recuperate has not been lost on subsequent writers.[110]

Sassoon was to write of Craiglockhart, which he called Slateford War Hospital, in his fictional autobiography *Sherston's Progress*:

> Outwardly, War Hospital was . . . elaborately cheerful. Brisk amusements were encouraged, entertainments were got up, and serious cases were seldom sent downstairs . . .[111]

> The doctors did everything possible to counteract gloom, and the wrecked faces were outnumbered by those who were emerging from their nervous disorders. But the War Office had wasted no money on interior decoration; consequently the place had the melancholy atmosphere of a decayed hydro, redeemed only by its healthy situation and pleasant view of the Pentland Hills. By daylight the doctors dealt successfully with these disadvantages, and Slateford, so to speak 'made cheerful conversation'.
>
> But by night they lost control and the hospital became

CRAIGLOCKHART HYDRO
NOW NAPIER UNIVERSITY

Richard Demarco 92

sepulchral and oppressive with saturations of war experience. One lay awake and listened to feet padding along passages which smelt of stale cigarette-smoke; for the nurse couldn't prevent insomnia-ridden officers from smoking half the night in their rooms, though the locks had been removed from all doors. One became conscious that the place was full of men whose slumbers were morbid and terrifying—men muttering uneasily or suddenly crying out in their sleep. Around me was that underworld of dreams haunted by submerged memories of warfare and its intolerable shocks and self-lacerating failures to achieve the impossible.[112]

It was at Craiglockhart that Owen wrote several of his best known poems including 'Dulce et Decorum Est', originally entitled 'Anthem for Dead Youth'. Sassoon was at Craiglockhart through the intervention of Robert Graves who had made various representations at the War Office. When Graves visited Sassoon in October 1917, Owen was not impressed, writing that he was 'a big, rather plain fellow, the last man on earth apparently capable of the extraordinary, delicate fancies of his books'. Soon after, Sassoon returned to England and Owen to the trenches, where he was killed a week before the Armistice.

Morningside was until the middle of the last century just a stopping point for farmers on the way to Edinburgh. James Grant in *Old and New Edinburgh* describes how in 1850 'a row of thatched cottages, a line of trees and a blacksmith's forge still slumbered in rural solititude'. It was the coming of the railway in 1872 that changed the whole district as wealthy citizens rushed to build villas in the sunny or 'morning side', southern part of the city.

Stevenson, in *Edinburgh: Picturesque Notes*, noted how:

the dismallest structures keep springing up like mushrooms; the pleasant hills are loaded with them, each impudently squatted in its garden, each roofed and carrying chimneys like a house. And yet a glance of an eye discovers their true character. They are not houses; for they were not designed with a view to human habitation, and the internal arrangements are, as they tell me, fantastically unsuited to the needs of man. They are not buildings; for you can scarcely say a thing is built where every measurement is in clamant disproportion with its neighbour. They belong to no style of art, only to a form of business much to be regretted.[113]

Morningside has a reputation for staid respectability and shabby gentility. Robert Kemp in his novel *The Maestro* captures something of the area in the following passage:

> In the district where the Urquhart-Inneses lived, all the houses resembled little castles and were enclosed by high garden walls topped with broken glass, so that anyone walking through the streets felt himself an outcast from society and hastened back to the pubs and narrow pavements at the east end of the city. . . . Not all these stately residences had been able to continue to play their pristine roles. One had a large brass plate to tell that behind these love-discouraging walls lurked St Devenick's School for Girls, another shamefacedly admitted to being the 'Brasenose Hotel, Open to non-residents', a third was Miss Newbattle's Nursing Home and a fourth the regional headquarters of the gas council.[114]

Though old ladies still inhabit huge rambling houses and can be seen shopping in their scarves, hats and bootees, younger families, many from the University or banking, have increasingly been moving in and houses have been divided into flats. In spite of that Morningside, with its manicured hedges, black iron railings and netted windows, remains the heart of old middle-class Edinburgh.

As one heads south down Morningide Road one can see on one's right, at No 112, a covered entrance leading to a rather forbidding eighteenth-century mansion. This is Bank House where Cosmo Lang, later Archbishop of Canterbury, spent his youth while his father was minister of the parish church opposite between 1868 and 1873.

Nearby at the top of Pitsligo Road is East Morningside House. This was the home of a writer whose work, while popular in her lifetime, has until recently fallen out of a favour. A wooden plaque on one of the gate piers has the simple inscription: Susan Ferrier (Writer). Born 7th September 1782. Died 5th November 1854.

Her first book *Marriage* published in 1818 earned her the title of 'Scotland's Jane Austen' and while perhaps too flattering a sobriquet, Ferrier's reputation as a satirist of early nineteenth century Edinburgh has grown over the last decade.

In 1982, to mark the bicentenary of her birth, the National Library of Scotland mounted an exhibition devoted to her life and work. The house is well worth a visit and apart from its permanent display of 'Ferrierana', visitors can see a willow tree in the garden which is said to have been grown from a cutting taken from Napoleon's garden at Longwood on St Helena.

Another Morningside writer whose work is now being reassessed is Tom MacDonald (1906–75). Though MacDonald, or as he preferred Fionn Mac Colla, was born in Montrose, he moved to Edinburgh in 1929, spending many years in Morningside Park. His novels *The Albannach* (1932), *And the Cock Crew* (1945) and *At the Sign of the Clenched Fist* (1967) deal with the repressive influence of Calvinism and the need for the growth of a genuine Scottish culture.

Another writer with similar nationalist preoccupations was George Campbell Hay (1916–84) who lived at 6 Maxwell Street until his death. A fellow contributor of his to *Four Points of a Saltire* (1970), together with Sorley MacLean and William Neil, was Stuart MacGregor (1935–1973) whose tragic death in a car accident in Jamaica at the age of thirty-seven robbed literature of a promising talent.

After training as a doctor at the University, where he was instrumental in founding the Folksong Society, MacGregor spent four years in the RAMC. His novels are largely set against the backdrop of university and medical life especially his largely autobiographical first book *The Myrtle and the Ivy* (1967). His second, more complex, novel *The Sinner* (1973) centres on the ideals and callings of the heart of an Edinburgh folk-singer, contemptuous of mid-Atlantic commercialised art and the gutlessness of Scottish politicians. MacGregor's *Poems and Songs* (1974) was selected by John Herdman.

Further down Morningside Road is Morningside Cemetery

which opened as the metropolitan cemetery in 1878. The occupants range from some of the leading Edinburgh figures over the last century to thousands of unknown people who died in the one-time City Poorhouse at Craiglockart.

One of the best-known people buried in the cemetery is Alison Cunningham, Stevenson's beloved nurse 'Cummy'. After leaving Swanston in 1893, 'Cummy' took a small flat at 23 Balcarres Street where she lived with a collection of dogs, all of whom died, it was said, from overfeeding. It was at Balcarres Street she was visited by a succession of Stevenson's admirers. Finally in need of constant care she moved in with a cousin at 1 Comiston Place, where she died in July 1913 aged ninety-one. She had outlived Stevenson by twenty years.

Returning to the Meadows one comes to Millerfield Place. The street takes its name from the engraver William Miller, who lived for many years in a huge house, Hope Park where he was visited by William Ruskin. Among the books that Miller illustrated were J. G. Lockhart's *Life of Sir Walter Scott* and John Brown's *Rab and His Friends*.

R. M. Ballantyne moved to 6 Millerfield Place in July 1866 after his marriage and was a regular attender at the nearby Chalmers Memorial Church. In 1878 he moved south to Harrow.

In the first volume of his autobiography, *Two Worlds*, the writer and critic, David Daiches (1912–), paints a portrait of this part of Edinburgh just after the First World War. The Daiches family moved to Millerfield Place in 1919 when Daiches' father became rabbi of the Edinburgh Hebrew Congregation, the two worlds discussed being the Scottish and Jewish.

The twin stone pillars at the east end of Melville Drive were erected by the Nelson publishing family, as a gift to the city. Between 1846 and 1878, when they were destroyed by fire, the firm, employing some 600 people, occupied premises at nearby Hope Park. Later they moved to Dalkeith Road, now also demolished.

John Buchan (1875–1940) worked for the firm between 1907 and 1929, brought in as literary adviser by Tommy Nelson, an old Oxford friend to whom he dedicated *The Thirty-Nine*

PRESTONFIELD HOUSE   Richard Demarco '9

Steps. For several months before his marriage in July 1907 he had made himself familiar with the publishing operation and the Buchans' first home was a Gothic villa at the foot of Arthur's Seat. Later when the Buchans visited Edinburgh they stayed with friends at 6 Heriot Row.

Buchan's responsibilities included the Nelson Sixpenny Classics and the Nelson Sevenpenny Library of copyright novels. He himself wrote several books for the firm, including a life of the Marquis of Montrose and a history of the First World War.

What however gave him most pleasure was his job as editor of a new magazine, the *Scottish Review*. This had been launched in April 1907 and did much, during the course of its two-year existence, to initiate a revival of interest in Scottish writing. In a letter to Lord Rosebery, he laid down his intention

> to deal fully with all interests, literary, political and social, with something Scottish in the point of view. We want to make it the centre of a Scottish school of letters such as Edinburgh had a hundred years ago.[115]

Buchan is now associated with popular thrillers such as *Greenmantle* and *The Thirty-Nine Steps*, but he was a writer of wide ability and had a tremendous interest in Scottish writing. He, for example, wrote the preface to Hugh MacDiarmid's first volume of poems, *Sangschaw*. MacDiarmid, not naturally sympathetic to a man like Buchan, some twenty years later was to call him 'Dean of the Faculty of Scottish Letters'.

To the east is Prestonfield House, a late seventeenth-century country house that is now one of the most elegant hotels in Edinburgh. When T.S. Eliot's *The Elder Statesman* was staged at the Royal Lyceum during the 1958 Festival he was a guest of honour at a reception at Prestonfield organised by Scottish PEN. Among the other guests were George Bruce, Sydney Goodsir Smith and Hugh MacDiarmid.

R. Scworlo '92   Duddingston Kirk

Edinburgh's Villages

Edinburgh is still a city of villages and nowhere is this more true than Duddingston, which nestles on the south side of Arthur's Seat. The Sheep Heid Inn apart from being an attractive, though overdressed, hostelry has many literary associations. The village is a popular spot at weekends, particularly because of its loch:

> in summer a shield of blue, with swans sailing from the reeds; in winter, a field of ringing ice. The village church sits above it on a green promontory; and the village smoke rises from among goodly trees. At the church gates, is the historical jougs, a place of penance for the neck of detected sinners, and the historical louping-on stane, from which Dutch-built lairds and farmers climbed into the saddle. Here Prince Charlie slept before the battle of Prestonpans; and here Deacon Brodie, or one of his gang, stole a plough coulter before the burglary in Chessels Court.[116].

Though it covers some thirty acres the loch is never more than ten feet deep. Since 1925 it has been a bird sanctuary, the reeds at the southern edge being especially suitable as breeding ground for birds.

It was at Duddingston that the sport of curling was invented and one of the most famous Scottish paintings is Henry Raeburn's picture of the Revd Robert Walker skating on the Loch. Stevenson leaves an evocative picture of a typical skating scene in *Edinburgh: Picturesque Notes*:

> The surface is thick with people moving easily and swiftly and leaning over at a thousand graceful inclinations; the crowd opens and closes, and keeps moving through itself like water; and the ice rings to half a mile away, with the flying steel. As night draws on, the single figures melt into

ARTHUR'S SEAT & ST. ANTHONY'S CHAPEL

Richard Demarco

the dusk, until only an obscure stir, and coming and going of black clusters, is visible upon the loch. A little longer, and the first torch is kindled and begins to flit rapidly across the ice in a ring of yellow reflection, and this is followed by another and another, until the whole field is full of skimming lights.[117]

Dominating the skyline is Arthur's Seat which Stevenson called 'a hill for magnitude, a mountain by reason of its bold design'. It is a popular place to go on those bracing walks the Scots love and many Edinburgh novels have scenes set on its slopes.[118]

Elspeth Davie in her novel *Coming to Light* (1989) provides a vivid description:

The city's ancient volcano could be seen for miles around. From such a distance it appeared as a misty, blue hill with a few dim, central hollows. Close up it was a fierce, dark-cliffed mountain with precipitous streams of red and black rocks below which were piled long screes of rusty gravel covered with patches of grass and wind-bent thorn bushes. Arthur's Seat was only one of many outbursts of vulcanism in Scotland. Its dim hollows could now be seen as dark basins where millions of years ago fires had spurted, where thundering ash and molten lava had filled the cavities and poured out over miles of the surrounding countryside. It stood high above the city—a dramatic landscape and a lonely one. Black and red sharp-edged cliffs rose above the path circling the hill, and beneath it, far below the steep scree slopes, one looked down upon formal white crescents, over criss-crossing roads between old houses, over spires and domes, and across to the stuborn knob of Castle Rock—that great plug of hard black basalt which had outlived a whole series of huge, primeval eruptions. Even the moving ice-sheets had not levelled it.[119]

Dorothy Wordsworth who climbed it during her Scottish tour in 1803 remembers sitting on a stone near the ruined St Anthony's Chapel:

overlooking a pastoral hollow as wild and solitary as any in the heart of the Highland mountains: there, instead of the roaring of the torrents, we listened to the noises of the city, which were blended in one loud indistinct buzz—a regular sound in the air, which in certain moods of feeling, and at certain times, might have a more tranquillizing effect upon the mind than those which we are accustomed to hear in such places. The castle rock looked exceedingly large through the misty air: a cloud of black smoke overhung the city, which combined with the rain and mist to conceal the shapes of the houses—an obscurity which added much to the grandeur of the sound that proceeded from it. It was impossible to think of anything that was little or mean, the goings-on of trade, the strife of men, or every-day city business—the impression was one, and it was visionary; like the conceptions of our childhood of Bagdad or Balsora when we have been reading *The Arabian Nights' Entertainments.*[120]

The composer Felix Mendelssohn, who spent a week in Edinburgh in July 1829 before going on to the Highlands, later wrote of the view from Arthur's Seat: 'Few of my Switzerland reminiscences can compare to this; everything here looks so stern and robust, half enveloped in haze or smoke or fog'. So impressed was Mendelssohn with Edinburgh that he later applied, unsuccessfully, for the Professorship of Music.

Encircling Holyrood Park is the Queen's Drive, a broad road about three and a half miles long from which there are some spectacular views of the city. Near the eastern exit from the Park is Muschat's Cairn. The Cairn marks the scene of an infamous crime in 1720 when Nicol Muschat, a surgeon, murdered his wife by cutting her throat after efforts at divorce and poisoning had failed. Originally the Cairn stood on Hunter's Bog, under Arthur's Seat, but was moved in 1822 so that George IV could see it without getting his feet wet.

The Cairn was also the clandestine meeting place of Jeanie Deans and her lover, the outlaw George Robertson in Scott's *Heart of Midlothian.*

In the book Scott gives us an excellent description of Salisbury Crags which, though it refers to 1736 could well apply now:

If I were to choose a spot from which the rising or setting
sun could be seen to the greatest possible advantage, it
would be that wild path winding around the foot of the
high belt of semicircular rocks, called Salisbury Crags, and
marking the verge of the steep descent which slopes down
into the glen on the south-eastern side of Edinburgh. The
prospect, in its general outline, commands a close-built,
high-piled city, stretching itself out beneath in a form,
which, to a romantic imagination, may be supposed to
represent that of a dragon; now, a noble arm of the
sea, with its rock, isles, distant shores, and boundary of
mountains; and now, a fair and fertile campaign country,
varied with hill, dale and rock, and skirted by the picturesque ridge of the Pentland mountains. But as the path
gently circles around the base of the cliffs, the prospect,
composed as it is of these enchanting and sublime objects,
changes at every step, and presents them blended with, or
divided from, each other, in every possible variety which
can gratify the eye and the imagination. When a piece
of scenery, so beautiful yet so varied—so exciting by its
intricacy, and yet so sublime—is lighted up by the tints
of morning or of evening, and displays all that variety of
shadowy depth, exchanged with partial brilliancy, which
gives character even to the tamest of landscapes, the effect
approaches near to enchantment.[121]

Portobello was until well into this century Edinburgh's
seaside resort, famous for its salt-water baths. Much had
changed however by the time Wilhelm de Geer, a Swede,
visited it in 1958.

The place looked lovely, fine sand, a gigantic complete
rainbow was arching like an aerial bridge from the shore
at the water's edge right across to the Fifeshire coast.
Under it on the sand, far out, thousands of gulls were
shining white in the dull light. The surface of the water
was smooth reflecting the sun with a silken sheen, in
spite of the calm you hear the ceaseless swishing of
the sea. In the north-east Inchkeith gives the effect of
a miniature Mont-Saint-Michel, so as long as you gaze
seaward everything appeals to your aesthetic sense.

But turn your glance towards terra firma! Ye gods and little fishes, what a sight! Factories, bathing pool, erections that look like unsightly outhouses, a ballroom, a relic from bygone ages. Where there are no buildings there is urban or suburban grass, mangy and dirty, that has grown out of broken-up ground. Now I begin to be suspicious even of the beach . . .[122]

Over the last decade attempts have been made to revitalise the town and its appearance is improving. Streets such as the nineteenth-century Brighton Place give some indication of how exclusive the town must once have been.

It was on the sands at Portobello that Walter Scott, the quartermaster of the Royal Edinburgh Volunteer Light Dragoons, used to exercise with his regiment. Scott had been instrumental in forming the Dragoons at the begining of 1797 after fears of a French invasion. In his full-dress uniform of scarlet coat with blue collar and cuffs, silver epaulettes, white breeches, black leather boots and spurs and helmet crested with leopard skin and red-and-white hackle he must have been a splendid sight.

Scott often stayed during the summer of 1827 at 37 Bellfield Street, a hundred yards from the beach. His son-in-law Lockhart had taken the house for the summer and the writer would come down to see his grandchildren, in particular 'Little Johnnie' for whom Scott was currently writing *Tales of a Grandfather*. The two-storey terraced house, with its neat front garden, is still there marked by a plaque.

At the top of Bellfield Street, in the High Street next to the Church of St Mark, was situated a detached two-storey villa called Shrub Mount. Here lived the essayist and geologist Hugh Miller (1802–56) for the last four years of his life and here he created a museum for his geological specimens.

Miller had been born near Inverness and came to Edinburgh as a young man to edit the *Witness*, the newspaper which became the voice of the Free Church. He wrote over forty books, of which the best known are *The Old Red Sandstone* (1841) and his autobiography *My Schools and Schoolmasters* (1854).

Two years later on Christmas Eve, in a fit of depression,

he shot himself in the study of his house. He was buried in the Grange Cemetery shortly after the burial of an Edinburgh gunsmith, Thomas Leslie, who had been accidentally killed while inspecting Miller's revolver. An opera based on Miller's life by Reginald Barnet-Ayres and Colin Maclean was performed at the 1974 Festival.

Leith has always been Edinburgh's port and until 1920 was a separate town. Alasdair Alpin MacGregor remembered in his autobiography how:

> A trip from Edinburgh to Leith in those days was equivalent to a visit to an entirely different town, though they were contiguous in the closest sense. The rivalry existing between them was considerable, though, to all intents and purposes, one scarcely could tell where the Scottish Capital ended, and her seaport began. From a departmental point of view, however, they were entirely separate communities, the one spurning the alleged amenities of the other. There were differences, too, that no schoolboy could fail to notice. The Leith bobbies wore dissimilar helmets (less expensive ones, we liked to think!) and the Leith bailies' lamps disported a different coat-of-arms. Leith's tramtrack was of a narrower gauge than ours, and the vehicles upon it correspondingly smaller. Yet, Leith was enjoying an electric system when Auld Reekie was still in the dark ages of traction by cable.[123]

Even now the divisions, despite the new-found prosperity of the town, remain. In Elspeth Davie's novel *Coming to Light* two of the central characters, Steve and Ben, feel more affinity with Leith than Edinburgh itself:

> Steve simply put the sea itself as his reason. No doubt it was a dirty sea, an oily sea down here, but it gave movement, even turbulence to the whole scene, unlike the formality of the city which could be both beautiful and rather forbidding. Down here the sky was fretted with the gesticulating shapes of old ships, and near the water were the cracked blocks from an ancient harbour wall. Behind new shops stood remains of the old—their

signboards scoured with half a century of salt. Old brass confronted new glitter. Even now Leith was a sombre place divided by strips of water-reflecting light, a black place with bands of newly-painted colour, a noisy place, but still dead silent in the lonely lanes between the vacant warehouses.[124]

Those vacant warehouses have now been turned into flats or restaurants. After years of being in large part derelict Leith now resounds to the sound of music and activity.[125]

Leith Links, still the main recreation area, have a number of literary associations. At one time they were notorious for the horse-racing that took place there, perhaps best commemorated in Robert Fergusson's poem about the Leith Races. In *The Expedition of Humphry Clinker* Matthew Bramble visits the racecourse at Leith. He goes on to describe what was then, and still is, the national sport:

> Hard by, in the fields called the Links, the citizens of Edinburgh divert themselves at a game called golf, in which they use a curious kind of bat tipped with horn, and small elastic balls of leather, stuffed with feathers, rather less than tennis-balls, but of a much harder consistence. This they strike with such force and dexterity from one hole to another, that they will fly to an incredible distance. Of this diversion the Scots are so fond, that when the weather will permit, you may see a multitude of all ranks, from the senator of justice to the lowest tradesman, mingled together, in their shirts, and following the balls with the utmost eagerness.[126]

At the corner of Claremont Road and Macdonald Road stands an imposing building, the former Broughton Junior Student Centre now Lothian Regional Council Property Services. The poet Christopher Murray Grieve, known as Hugh MacDiarmid (1898–1972), came here as a sixteen-year-old student teacher in 1908 from his native Langholm. Quickly he was drawn under the sympathetic wing of the Principal Teacher of English, George Ogilvie. Ogilvie, who became one of the most influential men in Grieve's life, has left a picture of the young poet:

I remember vividly Grieve's arrival among us. I see the little, slimly built figure in hodden grey, the small sharp-featured face with its piercing eyes, the striking head with its broad brow and great mass of flaxen curly hair. He hailed from Langholm, and had a Border accent you could have cut with a knife. I am afraid some of the city students smiled at first at the newcomer, but he very speedily won their respect. He certainly very quickly established himself in mine . . . He was not, it must be admitted, a model student; in some subjects, frankly, he had no interest. As a matter of fact he became the despair of most of his teachers. Yet none of them could help liking him. He had a most engaging ingenuousness, and I have yet to meet the infant who could look as innocent as Grieve.[127]

The atmosphere was a stimulating one for many of his student-teacher colleagues were also keen to write. These included Mary Baird Aitken, who after returning to Broughton to teach, published a novel *Soon Bright Day* about the Scottish radical Thomas Muir of Huntershill; Edward Albert, who wrote a number of novels based on episodes in Scottish history; and Roderick Watson Kerr whose volume of war poems *War Daubs* attracted some interest on publication. It was Kerr who, together with his fellow student John Gould and George Malcolm Thomson, in 1922 set up the Porpoise Press with the express intention of publishing Scottish poets and novelists. Among those to benefit were Lewis Spence, Neil Gunn and Grieve himself.

Grieve left Broughton just before the end of his three-year course. He claimed in his autobiography *Lucky Poet* that he had been forced to leave after the death of his father but his father in fact died eight days after Grieve's departure. The truth is more prosaic. Grieve had been involved in the theft of several books from his mentor, Ogilvie. Ogilvie anxious to avoid a scandal, allowed Grieve to resign on 27 January 1911, the school log recording that 'Christopher Grieve, Junior Student, resigned on grounds of health and mistaking his vocation'.

It was Ogilvie who helped Grieve obtain a job on the

Edinburgh Evening Dispatch but he was unhappy and lasted less than a year. The editor dismissed him on discovering that the young journalist had been supporting himself by selling review copies. The scandal was to have repercussions throughout his life. Grieve's application to join the *Scotsman* in 1920 was turned down because of it. Grieve had never been drawn to Edinburgh and he leapt at the chance to move to another job in journalism in South Wales.

Though he vowed never again to live in Edinburgh, Grieve did return briefly in 1918 to be married at 3 East Castle Road to Margaret Skinner, whom he had met five years before while working on the *Forfar Review* in Angus. For six months during the winter of 1932–33, before moving to Shetland, he travelled in from Longniddry to his job as Assistant Editor on the Scottish nationalist paper the *Free Man*, then based in India Buildings in Victoria Street.

A number of other writers have been educated at Broughton including the playwright and poet A. D. Mackie (1904-   ); J. K. Annand (1908-   ), who edited the *Broughton Magazine* and published MacDiarmid's early work; Fred Urquhart (1912-   ); and Alan Bold (1943-   ).

Pilrig House in Pilrig Street was the 'pleasant gabled house set by the walkside among some brave young woods' to which David Balfour went in Stevenson's *Catriona* in order to talk to James Balfour, advocate. Stevenson knew the area well and would often go to Leith Walk to consort with prostitutes or merely to escape the constrictions of his class. He must have been a strange sight in his blue-black flannel shirts, red tie, salt-and-pepper trousers and patent-leather shoes. He wrote warmly of such trips:

> I walk the streets smoking my pipe
> And I love the dallying shop-girl
> That leans with rounded stern to look at the fashions;
> And I hate the bustling citizen,
> The eager and hurrying man of affairs I hate,
> Because he wears his intolerance writ on his face
> And every movement and word of him tells me how
> much he hates me.

Pitrig House   Richard Demarco 92

I love night in the city,
The lighted streets and the swinging gait of harlots.
I love cool pale morning,
In the empty bye-streets,
With only here and there a female figure,
A slavey with lifted dress and the key in her hand,
A girl or two at play in a corner of waste-land
Tumbling and showing their legs and crying out to me
    loosely.

Another author who knew Leith Walk well was Thomas Carlyle who took it as the model for his Rue St Thomas de l'Enfer in *Sartor Resartus*. It was in Leith Walk he later claimed that he realised God did not exist.

Between 1822 and 1824 he lodged at 3 Spey Street (then called Moray Street) working on his Schiller translations and fighting off depression. The street, just off Pilrig Street, has been redeveloped but the house at the south-east corner looks very much like the sort of house he would have lived in.

Newhaven, further down the coast, has largely lost its identity but at one time it was a fishing port famous for its oysters and the fishwives in their colourful shawls. At the height of the oyster boom in 1886 six million oysters were landed, but overfishing meant that by this century the trade was dead. Herring continued into this century and the fisherwomen have been immortalised in Nathaniel Gow's song 'Caller Herrin' as well as Scott's *The Antiquary*.

Otherwise Newhaven has few literary associations. Scott docked there in 1832 before going on to Douglas Hotel and the Revd James Fairbairn, immortalised as the caring cleric in Charles Reade's *Christie Johnstone* (1853), broke from Newhaven Parish Church in 1843 to found his own Free Church.

Cramond, however, is full of associations going back to when it was a Pictish fort, and takes its name from the Gaelic for the fort on the Almond—*Caer Almond*. The Romans built a fort and harbour here as part of their defensive line stretching from the Forth to the Clyde. Later the village grew up around the mills built to service a succession of industries including grain, nail manufacturing and papermaking. Now

Richard Demarco 92   CRAMOND HOUSE.

it is reknown for its sailing and pretty, whitewashed quayside cottages.

Cramond was where the singing master Gordon Lowther in *The Prime of Miss Jean Brodie* lived, and where Miss Brodie used to spend her weekends in

> a large gabled house with a folly-turret. There were so many twists and turns in the wooded path leading up from the road and the front lawn was so narrow, that the house could never be seen from the little distance that its size demanded and it was necessary to crane one's neck upward to see the turret at all.[128]

Stevenson knew this area well. Cramond House is supposed to have provided the setting for his House of Shaws and he describes the village in chapter XXX of *St Ives*. It was while walking along the Cramond sea-shore towards South Queensferry that he told his father of his intention of becoming a writer.

With his friend Walter Simpson, the son of the famous doctor James Young Simpson, Stevenson often used to go canoeing in South Queensferry. It was with Simpson that Stevenson made his canoe trip through France, which became his book *Inland Voyage*.

The Hawes Inn at South Queensferry has a number of literary associations. It is where David Balfour is brought in *Kidnapped* by his uncle Ebenezer and handed over to Captain Hoseseason of the brig *Covenant*. The ship then sets sail for America with David aboard to be sold as a slave in the Carolina plantations. The inn is also where Lovel and Jonathan Oldbuck dine in *The Antiquary*.

A small residential street on the side of Corstorphine Hill makes an unlikely literary site. It was at Dinnieduff, 4 Hillview Terrace, that Helen Cruickshank (1886–1975) lived for over fifty years and where she entertained most of the members of the Scottish Literary Renaissance.

On coming to Edinburgh in 1912 to work as a civil servant, first in a branch of the National Health Insurance on Dean Bridge and then in the Old Commercial Exchange buildings in the Grassmarket, Cruickshank lodged in Marchmont

Crescent and then Shandwick Place. In the early 1920s she moved to Corstorphine about the same time she met Hugh MacDiarmid, an experience she later described as a 'watershed' in her life. MacDiarmid became a regular *habitué* of her spare room, the 'Prophet's Chamber', and with her was actively involved in promoting Scottish PEN, formed in 1927 at the instigation of Professor Herbert Grierson.

Cruickshank, herself a minor poet, was a friend and confidante to many writers including Edwin and Willa Muir, Lewis Grassic Gibbon, Norman MacCaig, Sydney Goodsir Smith, Donald and Catherine Carswell. MacDiarmid and Gibbon dedicated *Scottish Scene* (1934) to her. In 1973 she moved to Queensberry Lodge in the Canongate, where she died two years later.[129]

Colinton is remembered chiefly because of its associations with Stevenson. His maternal grandfather Lewis Balfour was the minister of Colinton Parish Church for thirty-seven years until his death in 1860 and Stevenson spent many holidays at the manse there. In later life he would remember

> It was a place in that time like no other: the garden cut into provinces by a great hedge of beech, and overlooked by the church and the terrace of the churchyard, where the tombstones were thick, and after nightfall 'spunkies' might be seen to dance at least by children; flower-pots lying warm in sunshine; laurels and the great yew making elsewhere a pleasing horror of shade; the smell of water rising from all round, with an added tang of paper-mills; the sound of water everywhere, and the sound of mills—the wheel and the dam singing their alternate strain; the birds on every bush and from every corner of the overhanging woods pealing out their notes until the air throbbed with them; and in the midst of this, the manse.[130]

It was here at the Manse, surrounded by scores of relations, that Stevenson was able to behave like any normal high-spirited young boy rather than the rather precocious child of the Edinburgh New Town.

The sixteenth century Colinton Castle, the ruins of which form part of Merchiston Castle School, was owned by among

Richard Demarco '92   Colinton MANSE

others George Drummond, the Lord Provost responsible for the building of the New Town, and Sir William Forbes of Pitsligo who married Walter Scott's sweetheart Williamina Stuart-Belsches. It is also the scene of Mrs Oliphant's famous ghost story 'The Open Door'.

Nearby is Bonaly Tower, which Henry Cockburn bought on his marriage in 1811 and then spent twenty years turning into a country seat. Like Scott at Abbotsford he assembled a collection of carved stones from old, dismantled buildings including the figure of Shakespeare from the original Theatre Royal at the east end of Princes Street.

Cockburn, who defended the wife of William Burke in the Burke and Hare case, was the great grandfather and great, great grandfather respectively of the writers Claud Cockburn and Evelyn Waugh.

Swanston also has numerous associations with Stevenson. The way to approach it is from Oxgangs Road and across the busy Edinburgh bypass. A track just before the village leads along to the eighteenth-century Swanston cottage which was the Stevenson family retreat from 1867 until 1880. Stevenson's father took the summer lease in the hope the country air would improve his son's health.

In his novel *St Ives* the hero Monsieur le Vicomte de Saint-Yves, after his escape from the Castle, makes for Swanston where he comes across a cottage that is the exact replica of the Stevenson home:

> A single gable and chimney of the cottage peered over the shoulder of the hill: not far off, and a trifle higher on the mountain, a tall old white-washed farmhouse stood among the trees beside a falling brook . . . a little quaint place of many rough cast gables and grey roofs. It had something the air of a rambling infinitesimal cathedral, the body of it rising in the midst two storeys high, with a steep-pitched roof and sending out up all hands (as it were chapter-houses, chapels and transepts) one-storeyed and dwarfish projections. To add to this appearance it was grotesquely decorated with crockets and gargoyles, ravished from some medieval church. The place seemed

hidden away being not only concealed in the trees of the garden, but, on the side on which I approached it, buried as high as the eaves by the rising of the ground. About the walls of the garden there went a line of well-grown elms and beeches, the first entirely bare, the last still pretty well covered with red leaves, and the centre was occupied with a thicket of laurel and holly in which I could see arches cut and paths winding . . .[131]

If one carries on up the original path past a three-sided square of grey one-storey buildings one comes to Swanston village:

The hamlet . . . consists of a few cottages on a green beside a burn. Some of them (a strange thing in Scotland) are models of internal neatness; the beds adorned with patch, the shelves arrayed with willow-pattern plates, the floors and tables bright with scrubbing or pipe-clay, and the very kettle polished like silver.[132]

The cluster of cottages with the grey window surrounds and the immaculate front gardens remain almost as Stevenson described them. Immediately above sheep graze contentedly and quite oblivious of the passing golfers while 'straight above the hills climb 1,000 feet into the air'.

At the highest point of the green there is a teak bench with the inscription:

To the Memory of Edwin Muir 1887–1959
Poet, Novelist, Essayist, Teacher.
This seat is given by his friends to
the village of Swanston where the poet
liked to linger and meditate.

Muir used to love coming up here and writes of his 'little paradise' in his poem 'In Love for Long'.

The Pentland Hills mark the southern limits of Edinburgh, and form this book's boundary. Stevenson knew them intimately. His first book was a sixteen-page pamphlet privately printed by his father called *The Pentland Rising* and towards the end of his life his thoughts again turned to what, from Samoa, he called the 'Hills of Home'.

SWANSTON GREEN   Richard Demarco '92

The year before he died he wrote to S. R. Crockett 'Do you know where the road crosses the burn under Glencorse Church? Go there and say a prayer for me.' The Church figures in *Weir of Hermiston*.[133]

Stevenson is perhaps the most elegiac and lyrical writer about Edinburgh, as well as its most distinguised representative. It is therefore appropriate that in any summing up about the city he should have the last word:

I was born likewise within the bounds of an earthly city illustrious for her beauty, her tragic and picturesque association, and for the credit of some of her brave sons. Writing as I do in a strange quarter of the world, and a late day of my age, I can still behold the profile of her towers and chimneys, and the long trail of her smoke against the sunset; I can still hear those strains of martial music that she goes to bed with, ending each day like an act of an opera to the notes of bugles: still recall with a grateful effort of memory, any one of a thousand beautiful and spacious circumstances that pleased me and that must have pleased any one in my half-remembered past. It is the beautiful that I thus actually recall, the august airs of the castle on its rock, nocturnal passages of lights and trees, the sudden song of the blackbird in a suburban lane, rosy and dusky winter sunsets, the uninhabited splendours of the early dawn, the building up of the city on a misty day, house upon house, spire above spire, until it was received into a sky of softly glowing clouds, and seemed to pass on and upwards by fresh grades and rises, city upon city, a New Jerusalem bodily scaling heaven.[134]

SWANSTON AND THE PENTLANDS   Richard Demarco '92

THE TRAVERSE THEATRE
JAMES COURT, LAWNMARKET

Richard Demarco 9

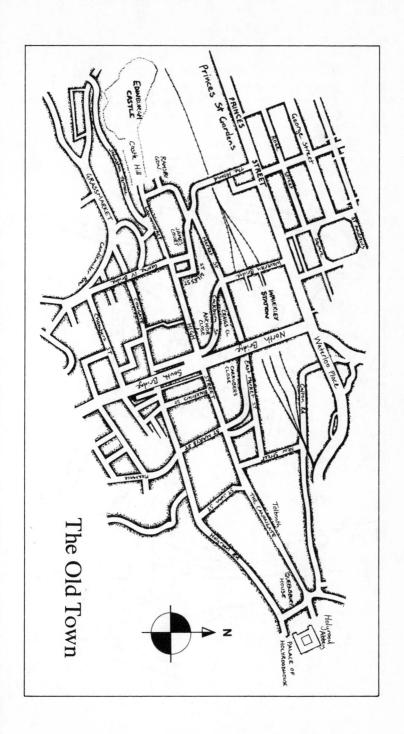

The Old Town

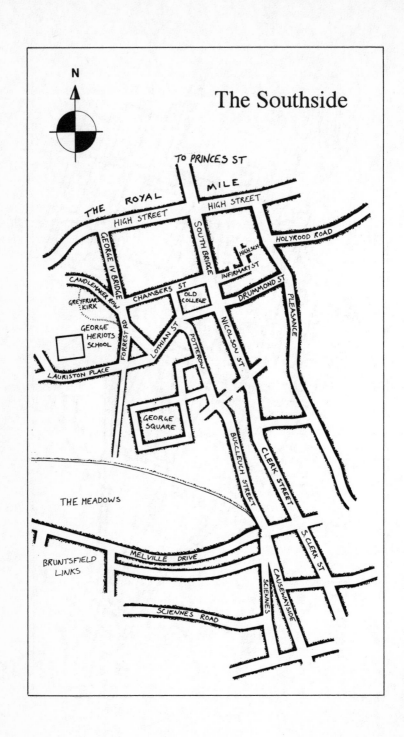

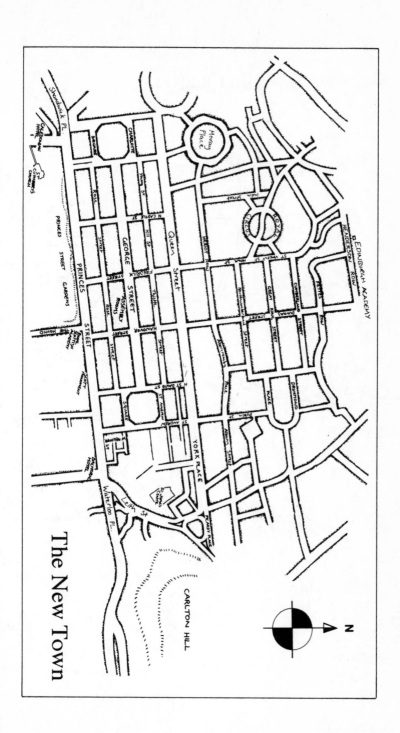

The New Town

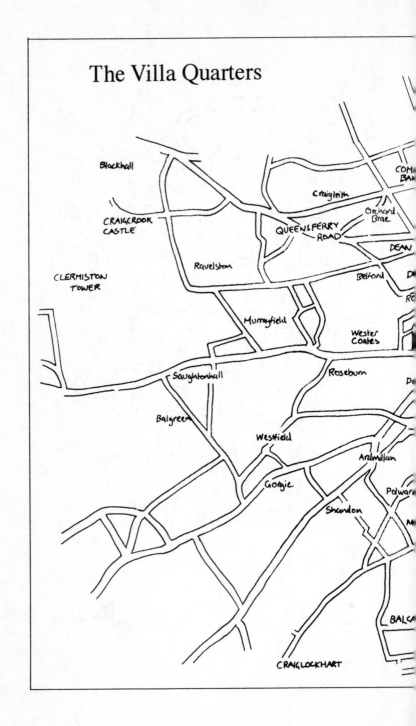

The Villa Quarters

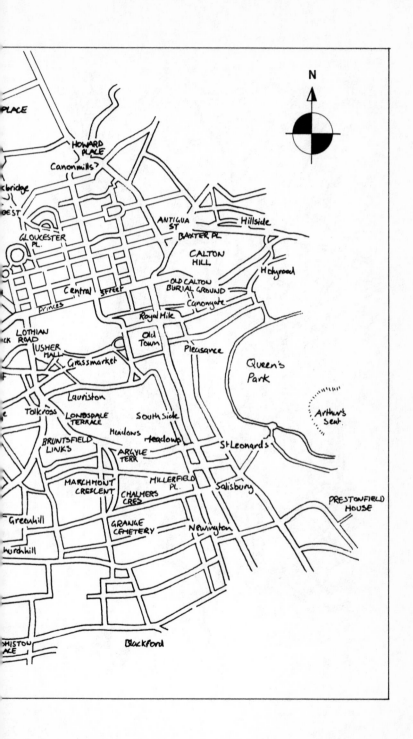

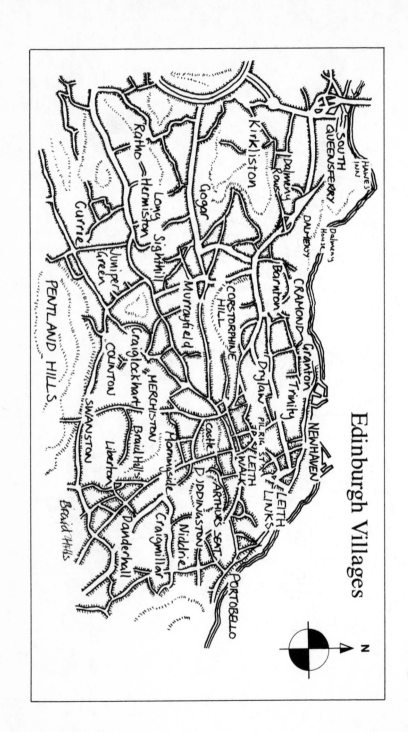

Edinburgh Villages

Reference Sources

THE OLD TOWN

1 Neil McCallum, *Scream in the Sky* (Cassell, 1964) p. 20.

2 A number of novels have scenes at Waverley. Eg Neil McCallum, *Scream in the Sky* (Cassell, 1964) p. 20; Simon Brett, *So Much Blood* (Gollancz, 1976) p. 9; Michael Bassi, *The Kilted Parrot* (The Molendivar Press, 1981) p. 9; James Allen Ford, *A Statue for a Public Place* (Hodder & Stoughton, 1965) pp. 173–174.

3 Quoted William Ruddick (ed), *Peter's Letters To His Kinsfolk* (Scottish Academic Press, 1977) Letter XXVII.

4 Quoted Rosaline Masson In Praise of Edinburgh (Constable, 1912) p. 205

5 Neil Gunn, *The Drinking Well* (Faber & Faber, 1946) p. 196.

6 For an investigation of the mystery which concludes that the infant is not James VI see Frank Gent, The Coffin in the Wall, *Chamber's Journal*, September and October 1944.

7 Robert Louis Stevenson, *St Ives* (Heinemann, 1898) p. 1.

8 George Borrow, *Lavengro* (John Murray, 1888) chapter 7.

9 John Gibson Lockhart, *The Life of Sir Walter Scott* (A & C Black, 1896) chapter XL.

10 Eric Linklater, *Magnus Merriman* (Cape, 1934) p. 138.

11 Owen John, *Festival* (Robert Hale, 1978) pp. 92–93. Simon Brett, *So Much Blood* (Gollancz, 1976) has a suicide from the Castle ramparts.

12 William Boyd, *The New Confessions* (Penguin, 1988) pp. 17–18.

13 Daniel Defoe, *A Tour Through the Whole Island of Great Britain*, GDH Cole (ed) (P Davies, 1927) p. 692.

14 G.K. Chesterton, *Robert Louis Stevenson* (Hodder & Stoughton, 1929) pp. 68–69. A good contemporary description of Brodie is given in Eric Linklater, *Edinburgh* (Newnes, 1960) p. 168.

15 Tobias Smollett, *The Expedition of Humphry Clinker* (OUP, 1985) p. 218.

16 Thomas Carlyle, *Reminiscences* (Longman, 1881) Vol 2, pp. 5–6.

17 Robert Louis Stevenson, *Edinburgh: Picturesque Notes* (Seeley & Co, 1900) pp. 52–53.

18 W. D. Lyell, *The Justice-Clerk* (William Hodge, 1923); James Allen Ford, *A Judge of Men*, (Hodder & Stoughton, 1968); Magda Sweetland, *The Hermitage*, (Macmillan, 1988).

19 Ruddick, *Peter's Letters to His Kinsfolk*, Letter XXVIII.

20 Muriel Spark, *The Prime of Miss Jean Brodie* (Penguin, 1965) p. 35.

21 Ibid. p. 108.

22 Smollett, p. 217.

23 Sir Walter Scott, *Heart of Midlothian* (OUP, 1982) pp. 56–57.

24 Henry Cockburn, *Memorials of his Time* (Robert Grant, 1945) p. 105.

25 Linklater, *Magnus Merriman*, p. 51.

26 See Neil McCallum's essay on Hogmany Traditions in *It's an Old Scottish Custom* (Dennis Dobson, 1951) pp. 15–22.

27 Cockburn, pp. 240–242.

28 For further information see W. M. Parker, *The House of Oliver & Boyd 1788–1948*, unpublished manuscript, Edinburgh City Library and George Bruce, *To Foster and Enrich: The First Fifty Years of the Saltire Society* (Saltire Society, 1986).

29 Alexander Carlyle, *Autobiography* (Foulis, 1910) p. 327.

30 Smollett. p. 222.

31 Letter to Craibe Angus. Quoted Neil McCallum, *A Small Country* (Mercat Press, 1983) p. 120. cf Robert Garioch's poem 'At Robert Fergusson's Grave'.

32 For a good description of Stewart see R. P. Gillies, *Reminiscences of a Literary Veteran* (Richard Bentley, 1851) vol 1 pp. 282–289.

33 For descriptions of the area see Boyd, p. 18 and Moray McLaren, *A Dinner With The Dead* (Serif, 1947), pp. 11–12.

34 Quoted Masson, p. 62.

35 Stevenson, *Edinburgh: Picturesque Notes*, pp. 6–8.

36 Quoted Michael Turnbull, *Edinburgh Portraits* (John Donald, 1987) pp. 86–87. Concerning the murder cf Rafael Sabatini's *The Night of Holyrood*, Algernon Swinburn's *Bothwell*. An opera with songs by Charles Dibdin was

performed at the Theatre Royal, Drury Lane in 1820.
Simon Brett's novel *So Much Blood* revolves around a
plot to bomb Holyrood.

37 Alexander Smith, *A Summer in Skye*, (Strahan, 1866)
pp. 19–20. Good descriptions can also be found in
Stevenson, *Picturesque Notes*, p. 39 and Alastair Alpin
MacGregor, *Auld Reekie* (Methuen, 1943) p. 137.

38 Joyce McMillan, *The Traverse Theatre Story 1963–1988*
(Methuen, 1988).

39 Accounts of the riot can be found in Scott, *Heart of
Midlothian*, and Carlyle, *Autobiography*, chapter 2.

40 A number of novels have been based on the story including
R. L. Stevenson's *The Body Snatchers*, I. Goodwin's *Bury
me in Lead* and Elizabeth Byrd's *Rest Without Peace*. cf
James Bridie's play *The Anatomist* and Dylan Thomas's
The Doctor and the Devil.

THE SOUTHSIDE AND UNIVERSITY

41 See William Watson, George Square 1766–1966, *University
of Edinburgh Journal* Spring 1966 vol XXII pp. 239–251.

42 Rebecca West, *The Judge* (Hutchinson, 1922) p. 74.

43 cf Sydney Goodsir Smith, Interim Report, *Gambit*, August
1957.

44 Cockburn, *Memorials*, pp. 25–26.

45 Lockhart, chapter 5.

46 9 Great King St; 1 Forres St; 29 Ann St, 113 Princes St and
71 Clerk St.

47 Their relationship has been the subject of many works of
fiction, most notably Robert Kemp's play *The Other Dear
Charmer*.

48 Stevenson, *Edinburgh: Picturesque Notes*, pp. 76–79.

49 A good portrait can be found in *Peter's Letters to His
Kinsfolk*, Letter X.

50 Donald Low, 'Walter Scott and Williamina Belsches', *Times
Literary Supplement*, 23 July 1971, pp. 865–866.

51 Quoted Andrew Pennycook, *Literary and Artistic Landmarks
of Edinburgh* (Charles Skilton, 1973) p. 82.

52 Smollett, p. 233.

53 *Letters of R. L. Stevenson*, vol 2, p. 276; *Letters of
R. L. Stevenson* vol 4, p. 274.

54 For a description of where 'The Spec' met see R. L.

Stevenson, *Memories and Portraits* (Richard Drew, 1990) pp. 46–47.

55 *Letters of R. L. Stevenson* vol 2, pp. 114–115.

56 Quoted Andrew Birkin, *The Lost Boys* (Futura, 1980) p. 24.

57 Arthur Conan Doyle, *The Firm of Girdlestone* (Chatto & Windus, 1890) chapter 5.

58 Conan Doyle, *Memories and Adventures*, p. 25.

59 Cockburn, *Memorials*, pp. 12–13. cf Borrow *Lavengro* 96–98.

60 Stevenson, *Edinburgh: Picturesque Notes*, p. 5. For another view see S. R. Crockett, *Kit Kennedy* (James Clarke, 1899) p. 296.

THE NEW TOWN

61 For descriptions of this 'split personality' see Linklater, *Edinburgh*, pp. 44–45 and Joan Lingard, *The Prevailing Wind* (Hodder & Stoughton, 1964) p. 47.

62 Ibid, p. 128.

63 Muriel Spark, What Images Return, in Karl Miller, ed *Memoirs of a Modern Scotland* (Faber, 1970) p. 151. The Balmoral figures in Ross, *The Edinburgh Exercise*, p. 29 and Moray McLaren, *The Pursuit* (Jarrolds, 1959) p. 204.

64 Ruddick, *Peter's Letters to His Kinsfolk*, Letter XLIV.

65 A recent study is David Groves, *James Hogg* (Scottish Academic Press, 1988)

66 A good description of the original Constable premises can be found in *Peter's Letters to His Kinsfolk*, Letter XLIII.

67 Cockburn, *Memorials*, pp. 104–105.

68 For a description of the Blackwood premises in Princes St., see *Peter's Letters to His Kinsfolk*, Letter XLIV. cf F Tredrey, *The House of Blackwood 1804–1954* (Blackwood, 1954).

69 53 Queen St until 1819 when he moved to 29 Ann St and finally from 1826 to his death 6 Gloucester Place.

70 James Allen Ford, *A Statue for a Public Place*, pp. 13–14.

71 Linklater, *Magnus Merriman*, p. 40.

72 Muir worked briefly for the British Council in Edinburgh lodging first at 47 Manor Place and then renting a flat at 8 Blantyre Terrace.

73 See Tom Driberg, *Ruling Passions* (Quartet, 1978) p. 144

for an account of how he was arrested for soliciting in the Gardens, an episode which he used in chapter XV of his novel about a homosexual politician *Thin Ice*.

74 W. M. Parker, Catherine Sinclair, *Edinburgh Tatler*, May 1967.

75 Quoted Pennycook, p. 83.

76 Ibid.

77 cf Patrick Chalmers, *Kenneth Grahame* (Methuen, 1933) and Eleanor Grahame, *Kenneth Grahame* (Bodley Head, 1963).

78 Smith, *A Summer on Skye*, p. 14.

79 Quoted W. Forbes Gray, The Edinburgh Relations and Friends of Dickens, *The Dickensian*, September and December 1926.

80 Tredrey, p. 192.

81 Quoted ibid, p. 168.

82 Quoted ibid, p. 186.

83 Alasdair Gray, *1982 Janine* (Cape, 1984) p. 282. The bar figures in Goodsir Smith's *Kynd Kittock's Land*, Abraham Adam's *Another Little Drink* and Norman MacCaig's poem *Milne's Bar*.

84 cf a portrait of Maclean in *Edinburgh University Alumni Magazine*, May 1990.

85 Hugh MacDiarmid, *The Company I've Kept* (Hutchinson, 1966), p. 233.

86 Alan Bold, *Hugh MacDiarmid*, (John Murray, 1982) p. 413.

87 Smith's final address was 24 Moray Place.

88 Linklater, *Magnus Merriman*, pp. 69–70.

89 For a description of the house see Morris Rosenblum, *The Baker Street Journal*, vol 13 no 4 1963. Conan Doyle's other addresses in Edinburgh include Liberton Bank House, 3 Sciennes Hill Place, 2 Argyle Park Terrace, 23 George Square and 15 Lonsdale Terrace.

90 Elizabeth Grant of Rothiemurchus, *Memoirs of a Highland Lady* (John May 1911) p. 284.

91 Moray McLaren, *The Capital of Scotland* (Douglas & Foulis, 1950) p. 64.

92 McLaren, *The Pursuit*, p. 148.

93 Ibid, p. 59.

94 Quoted Jenni Calder, *RLS: A Life Study* (Hamish Hamilton, 1980) pp. 16–17.

THE VILLA QUARTERS

95 Smith, *A Summer in Skye*, pp. 13–14.

96 See Robert Louis Stevenson, *Memories and Portraits*, pp. 149–158.

97 Linklater, *Edinburgh*, p. 53.

98 In Ian Miller's novel *School Tie* (Newnes, 1935), Sinclair College is based on Fettes.

99 See Andrew Kerr's pamphlet on Ann Street (1982), Edinburgh City Library and Elizabeth Hay, *Sambo Sahib* (Paul Harris 1981) p. 132.

100 Linklater, *The Merry Muse*, pp. 246–247 has a description of a suicide attempt from the bridge.

101 See Ruddick, *Peter's Letters to His Kinsfolk*, Letter VII for a contemporary description of Craigcrook.

102 Cockburn, *Memorials*, p. 282.

103 Quoted Wilmot Harrison, *Memorable Edinburgh Houses*, (Oliphant, Anderson & Ferrier, 1893) p. 75.

104 Novels with a Festival setting include Robert Blyth's *Festival*, Simon Brett's *So Much Blood*, Dorothy Halliday's *Dolly and the Singing Bird*, Owen John's *Festival* and Robert Kemps's *The Maestro*. A useful history of the Festival is George Bruce, *Festival in the North* (Robert Hale, 1975) while a more personal account is Owen Dudley Edwards, *City of a Thousand Worlds* (Mainstream, 1991).

105 Spark, *The Prime of Miss Jean Brodie*, p. 39.

106 Bruce Marshall, *The Black Oxen* (Constable, 1972) p. 19.

107 Smollett, p. 226.

108 Both Searle and Lee have written books about St Trinneans.

109 cf Hector Waugh, ed *George Watsons College 1724–1970* (1970).

110 A good recent example is Pat Barker's novel *Regeneration* (Viking, 1991).

111 Siegfried Sassoon, *The Complete Memoirs of George Sherston* (Faber, 1937) p. 638.

112 Ibid, pp. 679–680.

113 Stevenson, *Edinburgh: Picturesque Notes*, p. 118.

114 Robert Kemp, *The Maestro* (Duckworth, 1956) p. 45.

115 Quoted Royle, *Precipitous City*, p. 171.

EDINBURGH'S VILLAGES

116 Stevenson, *Edinburgh: Picturesque Notes*, pp. 156–159.

117 Ibid, pp. 159–160.

118 James Allen Ford, *A Judge of Men*; Jeremy Bruce Watt, *The Captive Summer* (Chambers, 1979) and Joan Lingard *The Prevailing Wind*.

119 Elspeth Davie, *Coming to Light* (Hamish Hamilton, 1989) p. 35.

120 Dorothy Wordsworth, *Recollections of a Tour in Scotland 1803* (Edmonstone & Douglas, 1874) p. 244.

121 Walter Scott, *Heart of Midlothian*, chapter 8.

122 Wilhelm de Greer, *Swede in Edinburgh* (William McLennan, 1965) p. 64.

123 Alastair Alpin MacGregor, *Portrait of a Lowland Boyhood* (Methuen, 1943) p. 92.

124 Davie, p. 100.

125 cf James Scott Marshall, *The Life and Times of Leith* (John Donald, 1986).

126 Smollett, pp. 225–226.

127 Quoted Bold, *Hugh MacDiarmid* (John Murray, 1989) p. 43.

128 Spark, p. 89.

129 cf Helen Cruickshank, *Octobiography* (Standard Press, 1976).

130 Robert Louis Stevenson, *Memories and Portraits* p. 76.

131 Stevenson, *St Ives* (Heinemann, 1899) pp. 46–47.

132 Stevenson, *Edinburgh: Picturesque Notes*, p. 174.

133 *Letters of R. L. Stevenson vol 2*, p. 288.

134 Quoted Penny Cook pp. 121–122.

Select Bibliography

Adam Smith, Janet *John Buchan* (OUP, 1985)
Adam Smith, Janet *John Buchan & His World* (Thames & Hudson, 1979)
Bamford, Francis *Edinburgh* (Faber, 1938)
Barclay, J.B. *Edinburgh from the Earliest Days to the Present Day* (A. & C. Black, 1965)
Barrie, J.M. *An Edinburgh Eleven* (Hodder & Stoughton 1896)
Benton, Jill *Naomi Mitchison* (Pandora, 1990)
Birkin, Andrew *The Lost Boys* (Futura, 1980)
Birrell, J.F. *An Edinburgh Alphabet* (The Mercat Press, 1980)
Bishop, Alan *Joyce Cary* (Michael Joseph, 1988)
Bold, Alan *Hugh MacDiarmid* (John Murray, 1988)
  Modern Scottish Literature (Longmans, 1983)
  Smollett (Vision, 1982)
  Muriel Spark (Methuen, 1986)
  Scotland: A Literary Guide (Routledge, 1989)
L. J. Brown and D. Forrest, *Letters of John Brown* (A & C Black 1907)
Bruce, George *Festival in the North* (Robert Hale, 1975)
  To Foster and Enrich: The First Fifty years of the Saltire Society (Saltire Society, 1986)
Buchan, Susan *John Buchan* (Hodder & Stoughton, 1947)
Calder, Jenni *A Robert Louis Stevenson Companion* (Paul Harris, 1980)
  RLS: A Life Study (Hamish Hamilton, 1980)
Cant, Malcolm *Villages of Edinburgh* (John Donald, 1986)
Campbell, Donald *A Brighter Sunshine: A Hundred Years of the Royal Lyceum* (Polygon, 1983)
Campbell, Ian *Thomas Carlyle* (Hamish Hamilton, 1974)
Carlyle, Alexander *Autobiography* (Foulis, 1910)
Carlyle, Thomas *Reminiscences* (Longman, 1881)
Catford, E.F. *Edinburgh: The Story of a City* (Hutchinson, 1975)
Chalmers, Patrick *Kenneth Grahame* (Methuen, 1933)

Chambers, Robert *Traditions of Edinburgh* (Chambers, 1868)

Chesterton, G.K. *Robert Louis Stevenson* (Hodder & Stoughton, 1929)

Cochrane, Robert *Pentland Walks: Their Literary & Historic Associations* (Andrew Eliot, 1908)

Cockburn, Henry *Memorials of His Time* (Robert Grant, 1945)

Cockburn, Harry *A History of the New Club 1787–1937* (Chambers, 1938)

Coghill, Hamish *Discovering The Water of Leith* (John Donald, 1988)

Cole, G.D.H. (ed) *A Tour Through The Whole Island* (Peter Davies, 1927)

Collie, Michael *George Borrow Eccentric* (CUP, 1982)

Collis, John Stewart *The Carlyles* (Sidgwick & Jackson, 1971)

Conan Doyle, Arthur *Memories & Adventures* (Hodder & Stoughton, 1924)

Cruickshank, Helen, *Octobiography* (Standard Press, 1976)

Daiches, David *Edinburgh* (Hamish Hamilton, 1978)
    Edinburgh: A Traveller's Companion (Constable, 1986)
    Walter Scott & His World (Thames & Hudson, 1971)
    Two Worlds (Canongate, 1987)

Darlington, W.A. *J.M. Barrie* (Blackie, 1938)

De Greer, Wilhelm *Swede in Edinburgh* (William McLennan, 1965)

Donaldson, Islay *Samuel Rutherford Crockett* (Aberdeen University Press, 1989)

Douglas, Hugh *Robert Burns* (Robert Hale, 1976)

Dunlop, Eilein & Kamm, Anthony *A Book of Old Edinburgh* (Macdonald, 1983)

Edwards, Owen Dudley *Edinburgh* (Canongate, 1983)
    The Edinburgh Stories of A. Conan Doyle (Polygon, 1981)

Fitzhugh, Robert *Robert Burns* (W.H. Allen, 1971)

Geddie, John *The Water of Leith from Source to Sea* (W.H. White, 1896)

Gillies, R.P. *Reminiscences of a Literary Veteran* (Richard Bentley, 1851 vol 1)

Gordon, Ian *John Galt* (Oliver & Boyd, 1972)

Grahame, Eleanor *Kenneth Grahame* (Bodley Head, 1963)

Grant, Elizabeth of Rothiemurchus *Memoirs of a Highland Lady* (Canongate, 1988)

Gray, Alasdair *Saltire Self-Portraits* (Saltire Society, 1988)

Gray, W. Forbes *An Edinburgh Miscellany* (Robert Grant, 1925)

Groves, David *James Hogg* (Scottish Academic Press, 1988)

Haight, Gordon (ed) *The George Eliot Letters vols 1–7* (OUP, 1954–56)

Hamilton, Alan *Essential Edinburgh* (Andre Deutsch, 1977)

Hammerton, J.A. *Barrie: The Story of a Genius* (Sampson Low, Marston, 1929)

Harris, Paul (ed) *Scotland: An Anthology* (Cadogan, 1985)

Harrison, Wilmot *Memorable Edinburgh Houses* (Oliphant, Anderson & Ferrier, 1893)

Hay, Elizabeth *Sambo Sahib* (Paul Harris 1981)

Holland, Lady *A Memoir of the Rev Sydney Smith* (Longmans, 1878)

Irving, Washington *Correspondence* ( )

Johnson, Edgar *Charles Dickens* (Allen Lane, 1977)

Jones, Ken *With Gold and Honey Blest: Edinburgh in Autumn* (Volturna, 1979)

Joyce, Michael *Edinburgh: The Golden Age 1769–1832* (Longmans, Green, 1951)

Lang, Theo *Edinburgh & the Lothians* (Hodder & Stoughton, 1952)

Lindsay, Ian *Georgian Edinburgh* (Oliver & Boyd, 1948)

Lindsay, Maurice *Robert Burns* (McGibbon & Kee, 1968)
    The Lowlands of Scotland (Hale, 1977)
    Scotland: An Anthology (Hale, 1974)
    The Scottish Renaissance (Serif Books, 1948)

Lindrop, Grevel *The Opium-Eater: A Life of Thomas De Quincey* (Dent, 1981)

Linklater, Andro *Compton Mackenzie* (Chatto, 1987)

Linklater, Eric *Edinburgh* (Newnes, 1960)
    The Man on My Back (Macmillan, 1941)
    A Year of Space (Macmillan, 1953)

Lochhead, Marion *Edinburgh Lore & Legend* (Robert Hale, 1986)

Lockhart, John Gibson *The Life of Sir Walter Scott* (A. & C. Black, 1896)

Lorimer, R.L. *Edinburgh: Scotland's Capital* (Oliver & Boyd, 1967)

MacCallum, Neil *It's an Old Scottish Custom* (Dennis Dobson, 1951)

McClevy, Alastair *The Porpoise Press 1922–39* (Merchiston Publishing 1988)

MacDiarmid, Hugh *Scottish Scene* (Jarrolds, 1934)

The Company I've Kept (Hutchinson, 1966)

MacGregor, Alasdair Alpin *Auld Reekie* (Methuen, 1943)
The Turbulent Years (Methuen, 1945)

McIntosh, Elspeth *Edinburgh* (Hale, 1987)

MacIver, Mary & Hector *Pilgrim Souls* (Aberdeen U.P., 1990)

Mackail, Denis *The Story of J.M.B.* (Peter Davies, 1941)

Mckean, Charles *Edinburgh: Portrait of a City* (Century, 1991)

Mackie, Albert *Edinburgh* (Blackie, 1951)

McLaren, Moray *The Capital of Scotland* (Douglas & Foulis, 1950)
Escape and Return (Chapman & Hall, 1947)
Return to Scotland (Duckworth, 1932)

Mair, William *Historic Morningside* (Macmillan & Wallace, 1947)

Magnusson, Magnus *The Clacken & the Slate* (Collins, 1974)

Marshall, James Scott *The Life and Times of Leith* (John Donald, 1986)

Martine, Roddy *The Lowlands and Borders of Scotland* (Michael Joseph, 1989)

Massie, Alan (ed) *Edinburgh and the Borders in Verse* (Secker & Warburg, 1983)

Masson, David *Edinburgh Sketches and Memories* (A. & C. Black, 1892)

Masson, Rosaline *In Praise of Edinburgh: An Anthology in Prose and Verse* (Constable, 1912)

Miller, Hugh *Edinburgh & its Neighbourhood* (Nimmo, 1889)

Miller, Karl (ed) *Memoirs of a Modern Scotland* (Faber, 1970)

Mitchison, Naomi *Small Talk: Memories of an Edwardian Childhood* (Bodley Head, 1973)

Moir, D.G. *Pentland Walks: Their Literary and Historical Associations* (Bartholomew, 1977)

Muir, Edwin *Scott and Scotland* (Routledge, 1936)
Scottish Journey (Heinemann, 1935)

Nimmo, Ian *Portrait of Edinburgh* (Robert Hale, 1975)

Oman, Carola *The Wizard of the North* (Hodder & Stoughton, 1973)

Parker, W.M. *The House of Oliver & Boyd 1788–1948* (Unpublished manuscript, Edinburgh City Public Library)

Parnell, Michael *Eric Linklater* (John Murray, 1984)

Pennycook, Andrew *Literary and Artistic Landmarks of Edinburgh* (Charles Skilton, 1973)

Rankin, Nicholas *Dead Man's Chest: Travels After Robert Louis Stevenson* (Faber, 1987)

Rosie, George *Hugh Miller* (Mainstream, 1981)

Royle, Trevor *A Diary of Edinburgh* (Polygon, 1981)
  Precipitous City: The Story of Literary Edinburgh (Mainstream, 1980)

Ruddick, William (ed) *Peter's Letters to His Kinsfolk* (Scottish Academic Press, 1977)

Sasson, Siegfried *The Complete Memoirs of George Sherston* (Faber, 1937)

Scott, P.H. *John Galt* (Scottish Academic Press, 1985)
  Walter Scott and Scotland (Blackwood, 1981)

Scott, Sir Walter *An Edinburgh Keepsake* (Edinburgh University Press, 1971)

Scott-Moncrieff, George *Edinburgh* (Batsford, 1947)

Simpson, E. Blantyre *Robert Louis Stevenson's Edinburgh Days* (Hodder & Stoughton, 1898)

Skinner, Robert T. *The Royal Mile* (Oliver & Boyd, 1947)

Smeaton, Oliphant *Famous Edinburgh Students* (Forbes, 1914)

Smith, Alexander *A Summer in Skye* (Strahan, 1866)

Smith, Charles J. *Historic South Edinburgh: vol 3* (Charles Skilton, 1986)
  Historic South Edinburgh vol 4 (Charles Skilton, 1988)

Smith, Sydney Goodsir (ed)*Robert Fergusson* (Nelson, 1952)

Steven, W. *History of the High School of Edinburgh* (Maclachlan, 1849)

Stevenson, R.L. *Edinburgh: Picturesque Notes* (Seeley & Co, 1900)
  Memories & Portraits (Richard Drew, 1990)

Thompson, Harold *A Scottish Man of Feeling* (OUP, 1931)

Topham, Edward *Letters from Edinburgh* (1776)

Tredrey, F.D. *The House of Blackwood 1804–1954* (Blackwood, 1954)

Turnbull, Michael *Edinburgh Portraits* (John Donald, 1987)

Wallace, Joyce M. *Historic Houses of Edinburgh* (John Donald, 1987)
  Traditions of Trinity and Leith (John Donald, 1985)

Ward, Robin *The Spirit of Edinburgh* (Richard Drew, 1985)

Watson, Roderick *The Literature of Scotland* (Macmillan, 1984)

Waugh, Hector (ed) *George Watson's College 1724–1970* (1970)

Williams, David *A World of his Own: The Double Life of George Borrow* (OUP, 1982)

Wilson, A.N. *Walter Scott: The Laird of Abbotsford* (OUP, 1980)

Wordsworth, Dorothy *Recollections of a Tour Made in Scotland AD 1803* (Edmonston & Douglas, 1874)

Yee, Chiang *The Silent Traveller in Edinburgh* (Methuen, 1948)

Appendix I

The following list comprises only the more important, evocative and recent of the several hundred novels with Edinburgh backgrounds. A complete record can be found in the Edinburgh Room of the Edinburgh Central Public Library arranged not in order of publication but of the chronological setting of the novel.

Baillie, Jamieson *Walter Crighton or Reminiscences of George Heriot's Hospital* (Livingstone, 1898)
Barker, Pat *Regeneration* (Viking, 1991)
Bassi, Michael *The Kilted Parrot* (The Molendinar Press, 1981)
Blyth, Robert *Festival* (Canongate, 1977)
Borrow, George *Lavengro* (OUP, 1982)
Bowen, John *The Truth Will Not Help Us* (Chatto & Windus, 1956)
Boyd, William *The New Confessions* (Penguin 1988.)
Bramble, Forbes *The Strange Case of Deacon Brodie* (Hamish Hamilton, 1975)
Brett, Simon *So Much Blood* (Gollancz, 1976)
Bruce–Watt, Jeremy *Captive Summer* (Chambers, 1979)
Buchan, John *John Burnet of Barns* (Canongate, 1979)
  A Lost Lady of Old Years (John Lane, 1899)
Byrd, Elizabeth *Rest Without Peace* (Macmillan, 1974)
Christie, Anna *First Act* (Piatkus, 1983)
Cost, March *After the Festival* (Cassell, 1966)
Craig, Robert *Traitor's Gait* (Porpoise Press, 1934)
Crampsey, Robert *The Edinburgh Pirate* (Canongate, 1979)
Crockett, Samuel Rutherford *The Black Douglas* (Smith, Elder, 1899)
  Kit Kennedy (James Clarke, 1899)
Davie, Elspeth *Climbers on a Stair* (Hamish Hamilton, 1978)
  Coming to Light (Hamish Hamilton, 1989)

Creating a Scene (Calder & Boyars, 1971)
De Quincey, Thomas *Confessions of an English Opium Eater* (OUP, 1985)
Douglas, Colin *The Greatest Breakthrough Since Lunchtime* (Canongate, 1977)
Douglas, Colin *The Houseman's Tale* (Canongate, 1975)
Doyle, Arthur Conan *The Firm of Girdleston* (Chatto & Windus, 1890)
Dunlop, Eileen *A Flute in Mayferry Street* (Richard Drew, 1987)
Ford, James Allen *A Judge of Men* (Hodder & Stoughton, 1968)
Ford, James Allan *A Statue for a Public Place* (Hodder & Stoughton, 1965)
Goodwin, I. *Bury me in Lead* (Alan Wingate, 1952)
Galt, John *Ringan Gilhaize* (Scottish Academic Press, 1984)
Gray, Alasdair *1982 Janine* (Jonathan Cape, 1984)
Gunn, Neil *The Drinking Well* (Faber & Faber, 1946)
Halliday, Dorothy *Dolly and the Singing Bird* (Cassell, 1968)
Hay, Ian *The Right Stuff* (Blackwood, 1908)
Hewlett, Maurice *The Queen's Quair* (Macmillan, 1904)
Hogg, James *Private Memoirs and Confessions of a Justified Sinner* (Canongate Classics, 1983)
Holland, Elizabeth *The House by the Sea* (Chatto & Windus, 1965)
   The House in the North (Macmillan, 1963)
Hunter, Mollie *The Lothian Run* (Canongate Kelpies 1984)
   The Spanish Letters (Canongate Kelpies, 1964)
John, Owen *Festival* (Hale, 1978)
Kemp, Robert *Gretna Green* Chambers, 1961)
   The Highlander (Duckworth, 1957)
   The Maestro (Duckworth, 1956)
   The Malacca Cane (Duckworth, 1954)
Kooning, Christian *A Mild Suicide* (Lime Tree, 1992)
Knox, Bill *A Killing in Antiques* (Hutchinson, 1981)
Lingard, Joan *The Gooseberry* (Hamish Hamilton, 1978)
   The Headmaster (Hodder & Stoughton, 1967)
   The Prevailing Wind (Hodder & Stoughton, 1964)
   The Second Flowering of Emily Montgomery (P. Harris, 1979)
   Reasonable Doubts (Hamish Hamilton, 1986)
Linklater, Eric *Magnus Merriman* (Cape, 1934 reissued by Canongate, 1990)
   The Merry Muse (Cape, 1959)

Lyell, W. D. *The House in Queen Anne Square* (Blackwood, 1920)
   The Justice–Clerk (W. Hodge, 1923)
McCabe, Brian *The Other McCoy* (Mainstream 1990)
McCallum, Neil *A Scream in the Sky* (Cassell, 1964)
McEwen, Todd *McX* (Secker & Warburg, 1990)
McGregor, Iona *An Edinburgh Reel* (Canongate, 1986)
MacGregor, Stuart *The Myrtle & the Ivy* (Macdonald, 1967)
MacGregor, Stuart *The Sinner* (Calder & Boyars, 1975)
McKelway, St Clair *The Edinburgh Caper* (Gollancz, 1963)
McLaren, Moray *A Dinner With the Dead* (Serif, 1947)
   (as Michael Murray) *The Noblest Prospect* (Duckworth, 1934)
   The Pursuit (Jarrolds, 1959)
Marshall, Bruce *The Black Oxen* (Constable, 1972)
   Father Malachy's Miracle (Heinemann, 1931)
   George Brown's Schooldays (Constable, 1946)
   Teacup Terrace (Hurst & Blackett, 1926)
Meek, James *McFarlane Boils the Sea* (Polygon, 1989)
Miller, Ian *School Tie* (Newnes, 1935)
Montgomery, K. L. *Major Weir* (Fisher Unwin, 1904)
Oliver, Jane *Not Peace but a Sword* (Collins, 1939)
   In No Strange Land (Collins, 1944)
Orr, Christine *Kate Curlew* (Hodder & Stoughton, 1922)
Pollatschek, Stefan *The Strange Story of John Law* (Hutchinson, 1936)
Pugh, Marshall *Stranger Any Place* (Hutchinson, 1962)
Rankin, Ian *Knots and Crosses* (Bodley Head, 1987)
   Hide and Seek (Barrie & Jenkins, 1991)
Reade, Charles *Christie Johnstone* (Sisley Books, 1907)
Ross, Angus *The Edinburgh Exercise* (Long, 1975)
Saxby, Jessie *Ben Hanson: A Story of George Watson's College* (Oliphant Anderson, 1884)
Scott, J.D. *The End of an Old Song* (Eyre & Spottiswoode, 1954 reissued by Canongate, 1990)
Scott, Sir Walter *The Abbot* (Nelson, 1938)
   Guy Mannering (Soho, 1987)
   The Heart of Midlothian (OUP, 1982)
   Redgauntlet (Nelson, 1938)
   Waverley (OUP, 1986)
Scott–Moncrieff, George *Burke Street* (Richard Patterson, 1956)
   Tinker's Wind (Wishart, 1933)
Sinclair, Catherine *Holiday House* (Garland, 1976)

Smith, Sydney Goodsir *Carotid Cornucopius* (Macdonald, 1964)

Smollett, Tobias *The Expedition of Humphry Clinker* (OUP, 1984)

Spark, Muriel *The Prime of Miss Jean Brodie* (Penguin, 1965)

Stevenson, Robert Louis *Dr Jeykll and Mr Hyde* and *The Bodysnatcher* (OUP, 1990)
   Catriona (Canongate, 1989)
   'The Misadventures of John Nicholson' in *The Scottish Stories and Essays*, Kenneth Gelder (ed) (Edinburgh University Press, 1989)
   St Ives (Heinemann, 1898)
   Weir of Hermiston (Penguin, 1979)

Swan, Annie *Adam Hepburn's Vow* (Cassell, 1885)

Sweetland, Magda, *Eightsome Reel* (Macmillan, 1985)
   The Hermitage (Macmillan, 1988)

Taylor, Vincent *Sunray* (Macdonald, 1982)

Thomson, George Malcolm *The Ball at Glenkevan* (Secker & Warburg, 1982)

Urquhart, Fred *Palace of Green Days* (Quartet, 1979)
   Time Will Knit (Richard Drew, 1988)

West, Rebecca *The Judge* (Hutchinson, 1922)

Appendix II

EDINBURGH LITERARY FIGURES

WILLIAM EDMONDSTOUNE AYTOUN (1813–65). Son-in-law of John Wilson, he is best remembered for his humourous short stories and satirical verse parodies.

R. M. BALLANTYNE (1825–94). Wrote adventure novels, of which the best known is *Coral Island* (1858).

HELEN BANNERMAN (1862–1946). The author of *Little Black Sambo* was born and educated in the city, returning to spend almost thirty years of her retirement there.

J. M. BARRIE (1860–1937). One of the Kailyard school of writers, now largely remembered for his plays *Peter Pan* and *The Admirable Crichton*.

WILLIAM BLACKWOOD (1776–1834). Publisher, who founded Tory *Blackwood's Magazine* in opposition to Whig *Edinburgh Review*.

ALAN BOLD (1943–   ). Prodigious writer, journalist and poet often associated with the older members of the Scots Literary Renaissance.

GEORGE BORROW (1803–81). His best known book *Lavengro* is based on his early life in Edinburgh.

JAMES BOSWELL (1740–95). Best known for his biography of Samuel Johnson and *The Journal of the Tour to the Hebrides*.

JOHN BUCHAN (1875–1940). Lived and worked in Edinburgh returning as Lord High Commissioner.

GEORGE BUCHANAN (1506–82). A scholar and translator, he also wrote plays, poetry and a history of Scotland.

ROBERT BURNS (1759–96). Scotland's premier poet. During his two visits to Edinburgh he wrote some of his most famous poems and had his famous correspondence with 'Clarinda'.

ALEXANDER 'JUPITER' CARLYLE (1722–1805). His *Autobiography* provides a vivid picture of Scottish life during the late eighteenth century.

THOMAS CARLYLE (1795–1881). Writer and historian, whose best known books are *The French Revolution* and *Sartor Resartus*.

JOYCE CARY (1888–1957). Author of *The Horse's Mouth* and *Mr Johnson*, his first book was published while at Edinburgh Art School.

HENRY COCKBURN (1779–1854). Solicitor General and contributor to *The Edinburgh Review*, his *Memorials of His Time* is a classic account of Edinburgh society during the first half of the nineteenth century. Great, great grandfather of Evelyn Waugh.

ARCHIBALD CONSTABLE (1774–1827). Publisher of *The Edinburgh Review* and Sir Walter Scott.

WILLIAM CREECH (1745–1815). Lord Provost and publisher of Robert Burns.

HELEN CRUICKSHANK (1886–1975). Though a poet in her own right, she is now remembered for her support of Scottish PEN and writers like Hugh MacDiarmid.

DAVID DAICHES (1912–   ). Distinguished academic who has written widely about Edinburgh's history and literary figures.

DANIEL DEFOE (1660–1731). The author of *Robinson Crusoe* lived in Edinburgh in 1707 and returned in 1724 on his *Tour Through the Whole Island*.

CHARLES DICKENS (1812–70). His wife's family came from Edinburgh and the novelist made a number of successful reading tours to the city.

ARTHUR CONAN DOYLE (1859–1930). He wrote a number of stories based on his youth in the capital and Sherlock Holmes was supposedly based on one of his teachers at the University.

WILLIAM DRUMMOND (1585–1649). Probably the most important Scottish literary figure of the 17th century. He lived just outside Edinburgh.

GEORGE ELIOT (1819–80). Visited Edinburgh in 1845 and 1852.

ROBERT FERGUSSON (1750–74). Poet who wrote about ordinary people and life in Edinburgh, much admired by Burns and Stevenson.

SUSAN FERRIER (1782–1854). One of Edinburgh's few nineteenth century female novelists, she is often generously compared to Jane Austen.

JOHN GALT (1779–1839). Novelist whose work tended to trade on the Scottish nostalgia boom created by Scott.

ROBERT GARIOCH (1909–82). One of the most distinguished Edinburgh poets of the twentieth century.

JOHN GAY (1685–1732). The poet and playwright spent some
time in Edinburgh.

OLIVER GOLDSMITH (1728–74). The author of *The Vicar
of Wakefield* studied medicine at the University and
subsequently wrote about the city's dancing assemblies.

KENNETH GRAHAME (1859–1932). The author of *The Wind in
the Willows* was born and spent the first few years of his life
in Edinburgh, without any noticeable effect on his writing.

ALASDAIR GRAY (1935–). Though strictly speaking a
Glasgow writer, his novel *1982 Janine* has some marvellous
Edinburgh scenes.

C. M. GRIEVE (1892–1978). As Hugh MacDiarmid a leading
figure in the Scots Literary Renaissance of the twentieth
century. His most famous poem is *A Drunk Man Looks at
the Thistle*.

NEIL GUNN (1891–1973). Worked for the Civil Service in
Edinburgh 1909–11 and writes about the city in his novel
The Drinking Well.

W. E. HENLEY (1849–1903). Friend and collaborator with
R.L. Stevenson and J.M. Barrie. He supposedly was the
inspiration for Long John Silver and his daughter for Wendy
in *Peter Pan*.

JAMES HOGG (1770–1835). Known as *The Ettrick Shepherd* and
a friend of Scott, his most important book is *The Private
Memoirs and Confessions of a Justified Sinner*.

JOHN HOME (1722–1808). A minister whose play *Douglas*
aroused opposition from colleagues in the Church thereby
further delaying the establishment of a Scottish theatrical
tradition.

DAVID HUME (1711–76). Major figure of the Scottish
Enlightenment, who challenged in a series of books hitherto
sacrosanct beliefs about religion and argued for the power of
reason.

HENRY JAMES (1843–1916). A friend of Stevenson, he visited
Edinburgh in 1876.

FRANCIS JEFFREY (1773–1850). Lord Advocate and
first editor of *The Edinburgh Review*. He wrote the
inscription for the foundation stone of the Scott
Monument.

DR SAMUEL JOHNSON (1709–84). Visited Edinburgh in 1771
and was highly critical of the city.

JOHN KNOX (1505–72). Writer and preacher whose influence

on the intellectual, social and religious life of the city has
lasted to the present day.

ERIC LINKLATER (1899–1974). Novelist and Scottish Nationalist
who wrote a number of books about, or set in, Edinburgh.

JOHN GIBSON LOCKHART (1794–1854). Son-in-law and
biographer of Sir Walter Scott, he also wrote several novels
and a series of sketches on Scottish life *Peter's Letters to his
Kinsfolk*.

NORMAN MacCAIG (1910–). Probably Edinburgh's most
famous living poet.

DUNCAN BAN MCINTYRE (1724–1812). Though reknown for
his Gaelic poetry, half his life was spent in Edinburgh.

COMPTON MACKENZIE (1883–1974). Prolific writer, often
about himself, now principally remembered for his novel
Whisky Galore.

SIR GEORGE MACKENZIE (1636–91). Founder of the Advocates'
Library, he wrote Scotland's first novel as well as several
books of law, history and poetry.

HENRY MACKENZIE (1754–1831). Lionized in his lifetime for
his novel *The Man of Feeling*, his significance in retrospect is
as a patron of Burns and elder statesman of the arts.

MORAY McLAREN (1901–71). Novelist who lived for many
years in Inverleith Row.

SORLEY MACLEAN (1911–). Scotland's greatest living Gaelic
poet was educated, and then taught for several years, in
the city.

BRUCE MARSHALL (1899–). Author of several satirical novels
about Edinburgh, most notably *The Black Oxen*.

HUGH MILLER (1802–56). Geologist and essayist, who
embodied the independence of the Scottish dissenting
tradition.

NAOMI MITCHISON (1897–). Born in Edinburgh
and author of countless books ranging from science
fiction to feminism, she is also a Chief of a Botswanan
tribe.

EDWIN MUIR (1887–1959). Poet and stringent critic of
Edinburgh, best exemplified in *Scottish Journey*.

WILFRID OWEN (1893–1918). While convalescing in
Craiglockhart Hospital wrote some of his most memorable
poetry.

THOMAS DE QUINCEY (1785–1859). Spent the last forty years
of his life in debt and in various lodgings around the city,

where he wrote his masterpiece *Confessions of an English Opium Eater*.

ALLAN RAMSAY (1685–1758). Poet, publisher and founder of Edinburgh's first lending library.

JOHN RUSKIN (1819–1900). A frequent visitor to, and highly critical of, the New Town, much of his work was published in *The Edinburgh Review*.

SIEGFRIED SASSOON (1886–1967). First World War poet, who spent several months at Craiglockhart hospital.

WALTER SCOTT (1771–1832). Born, educated and most of his life resident in Edinburgh, he drew on the city and its history for many of his novels, with the result he is probably the pre-eminent Edinburgh literary figure of all time.

PERCY BYSSHE SHELLEY (1792–1822). Paid visits to the city in 1811 and 1813, marrying the same person on each occasion.

CATHERINE SINCLAIR (1800–64). One of the most successful novelists of her day, she supposedly first guessed the identity of *The Great Unknown*.

ADAM SMITH (1723–90). Another major figure of the Scottish Enlightenment, who as a result of his *Inquiry into the Nature and Causes of the Wealth of Nations* is regarded as the founder of the modern study of political economy.

SYDNEY GOODSIR SMITH (1915–75). Poet and novelist whose *Carotid Cornucopius* celebrates the capital, much as his hero Robert Fergusson did two centuries before.

WILLIAM SMELLIE (1740–95). Friend of Burns and as editor of *The Encyclopaedia Britannica* made an important contribution to the Scottish Enlightenment.

TOBIAS SMOLLETT (1721–71). Wrote *The Expedition of Humphry Clinker*, which has many scenes set in Edinburgh while staying with his sister in the city.

MURIEL SPARK (1918–   ). Though choosing to exile herself from Edinburgh at an early age her novel *The Prime of Miss Jean Brodie* is one of the best realisations of the city and its social nuances.

LEWIS SPENCE (1874–1955). Poet who championed the cause of writing in Scots.

ROBERT LOUIS STEVENSON (1850–94). Major writer whose life has sometimes overshadowed his writing, much of which is about the city in which he was born.

DUGALD STEWART (1753–1828). Professor of moral

philosophy and influential figure of the Scottish
Enlightenment.

WILLIAM THACKERAY (1811–63). Came to the city several
times on lecture tours despite being hissed on an early visit.

FRED URQUHART (1912–   ). Novelist and short story writer
who draws on his Edinburgh childhood for some of
his work.

JOHN WESLEY (1703–91). Preached several times on Calton
Hill and leaves a picture of the city during the eighteenth
century in his diaries.

REBECCA WEST (1892–1983). Though she left the city as a child
she gives a sharp portrait of the city in her novel *The Judge*.

JOHN WILSON (1785–1854). Author of the *Noctes Ambrosianae*
for Blackwoods, he was also one of the first critics to do
justice to Wordsworth.

WILLIAM WORDSWORTH (1770–1850). Came to Edinburgh in
1803, during which he paid a visit to Scott in Lasswade.

Index